HIKE THE PARKS

JOSHUA TREE
NATIONAL PARK

HIKE THE PARKS

BEST DAY HIKES, WALKS, AND SIGHTS

JOSHUA TREE
NATIONAL PARK

SCOTT TURNER

MOUNTAINEERS
BOOKS

For Peep and Bonez

MOUNTAINEERS BOOKS is dedicated to the exploration, preservation, and enjoyment of outdoor and wilderness areas.

1001 SW Klickitat Way, Suite 201, Seattle, WA 98134
800-553-4453, www.mountaineersbooks.org

Printed in China
Distributed in the United Kingdom by Cordee, www.cordee.co.uk

First edition, 2019

Copyeditor: Erin Cusick
Design: Jen Grable
Layout: McKenzie Long
Cartographer: Lohnes+Wright
All photographs by the author unless credited otherwise
Cover photographs, front: *A Joshua tree cast in silhouette by the rising sun;* back: *Gardens of pinnacles in the Jumbo Rocks area*
Frontispiece: *Dawn's rosy fingers caress Mount San Gorgonio.*
Last page: *Rays of light cascade over the Coachella Valley.*

Library of Congress Cataloging-in-Publication data is on file for this title at https://lccn.loc.gov/2018053943

Mountaineers Books titles may be purchased for corporate, educational, or other promotional sales, and our authors are available for a wide range of events. For information on special discounts or booking an author, contact our customer service at 800-553-4453 or mbooks@mountaineersbooks.org.

Printed on FSC®-certified materials

ISBN (paperback): 978-1-68051-252-6
ISBN (ebook): 978-1-68051-253-3

MIX
Paper from responsible sources
FSC® C008047
www.fsc.org

An independent nonprofit publisher since 1960

CONTENTS

BLACK ROCK CANYON

WEST ENTRANCE

LOST HORSE VALLEY

OPPOSITE *Weaving and wending on the way to Willow Hole (Route 11)*

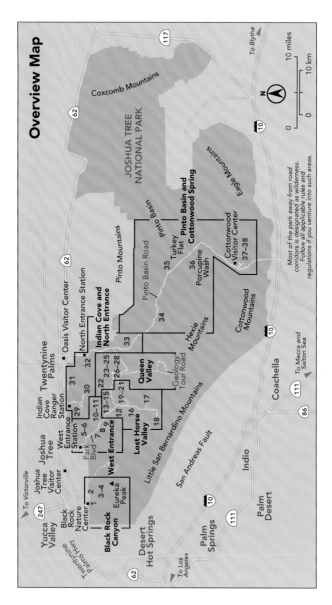

Overview Map

JOSHUA TREE NATIONAL PARK

Coxcomb Mountains

Eagle Mountains

Pinto Mountains

Pinto Basin

Pinto Basin Road

35 Turkey Flat

Pinto Basin and Cottonwood Spring

36 Porcupine Wash

34

Hexie Mountains

Cottonwood Mountains

Cottonwood Visitor Center

37–38

To Blythe

To Mecca and Salton Sea

Coachella

Cottonwood

Oasis Visitor Center

North Entrance Station

Indian Cove and North Entrance

Twentynine Palms

Indian Cove Ranger Station

33

32

31

30

29

Queen Valley

Geology Tour Road

23–25

26–28

22

19–21

17

16

18

10–11

13–15

12

Lost Horse Valley

Little San Bernardino Mountains

San Andreas Fault

Joshua Tree

West Entrance Station

Park Blvd

5–6

7 8 9

West Entrance

Joshua Tree Visitor Center

Black Rock Nature Center

1 2

3–4

Eureka Peak

Black Rock Canyon

Yucca Valley

Twentynine Palms Hwy

Desert Hot Springs

To Victorville

To Los Angeles

Palm Springs

Palm Desert

Indio

Coachella

Most of the park away from road corridors is designated as wilderness. Follow all applicable rules and regulations if you venture into such areas.

N

0   10 miles

0   10 km

247

62

62

62

117

111

111

86

10

10

10

8

HIKES AT A GLANCE

	HIKE	DISTANCE miles (km)	ELEVATION GAIN feet (m)	HIGH POINT feet (m)	DIFFICULTY
BLACK ROCK CANYON					
1.	High View Nature Trail	1.3 (2.1)	350 (115)	4477 (1365)	Easy
2.	Eureka Peak	9.6 (15.4)	1850 (565)	5518 (1682)	Challenging
3.	Warren Peak	5.2 (8.4)	1090 (335)	5103 (1555)	Moderate
4.	Panorama Loop	5.9 (9.5)	1200 (365)	5195 (1583)	Moderate
WEST ENTRANCE					
5.	North View Trail	5.1 (8.2)	1070 (325)	4437 (1352)	Moderate
6.	Maze-Windows Loop	5.9 (9.5)	680 (210)	4270 (1300)	Moderate
7.	Bigfoot-Panorama Loop	7 (11.3)	1400 (425)	4269 (1301)	Challenging
8.	Quail Mountain	10.2 (16.4)	2600 (790)	5813 (1772)	Strenuous
9.	Johnny Lang Canyon	6 (9.7)	630 (190)	4342 (1324)	Challenging
10.	Boy Scout Trail	8 (12.9)	375 (115)	4185 (1275)	Challenging
11.	Willow Hole	7 (11.3)	300 (90)	4163 (1269)	Moderate
LOST HORSE VALLEY					
12.	Hidden Valley Nature Trail	1 (1.6)	150 (45)	4269 (1301)	Easy

HIKE	DISTANCE miles (km)	ELEVATION GAIN feet (m)	HIGH POINT feet (m)	DIFFICULTY
13. Barker Dam	1.3 (2.1)	115 (35)	4295 (1310)	Easy
14. Wonderland of Rocks	3.6 (5.8)	250 (75)	4528 (1380)	Challenging
15. Wall Street Mill	1.5 (2.4)	100 (30)	4351 (1326)	Easy
16. Cap Rock Nature Trail	0.4 (0.6)	25 (8)	4268 (1301)	Easy
17. Lost Horse Mine	6.7 (10.8)	1000 (305)	5113 (1558)	Challenging
18. Inspiration Peak	1.9 (3.1)	850 (260)	5578 (1700)	Moderate
19. Ryan Ranch	1.1 (1.8)	90 (30)	4368 (1331)	Easy
20. Hall of Horrors	1.1 (1.8)	70 (20)	4341 (1323)	Easy
21. Ryan Mountain	2.8 (4.5)	1050 (320)	5457 (1663)	Moderate
QUEEN VALLEY				
22. Queen Mountain	4 (6.4)	1200 (365)	5682 (1732)	Strenuous
23. Pine City	4 (6.4)	230 (70)	4575 (1395)	Moderate
24. Desert Queen Mine	1.5 (2.4)	300 (90)	4462 (1360)	Moderate
25. Lucky Boy Loop	3.5 (5.6)	250 (75)	4525 (1379)	Moderate
26. Skull Rock Nature Trail	1.7 (2.7)	230 (70)	4369 (1332)	Easy
27. Discovery Nature Trail	0.8 (1.3)	110 (35)	4350 (1325)	Easy
28. Split Rock	1.9 (3.1)	350 (105)	4369 (1332)	Easy

HIKE	DISTANCE miles (km)	ELEVATION GAIN feet (m)	HIGH POINT feet (m)	DIFFICULTY
INDIAN COVE AND NORTH ENTRANCE				
29. Indian Cove Nature Trail	0.6 (1)	70 (20)	3356 (1023)	Easy
30. Rattlesnake Canyon	2.2 (3.5)	500 (150)	3413 (1040)	Challenging
31. Fortynine Palms Oasis	3 (4.8)	750 (230)	3075 (935)	Challenging
32. Contact Mine	3.8 (6.1)	725 (220)	3628 (1106)	Moderate
33. Arch Rock Nature Trail	0.5 (0.8)	50 (15)	3845 (1170)	Easy
PINTO BASIN AND COTTONWOOD SPRING				
34. Cholla Cactus Garden	0.3 (0.5)	Negligible	2202 (671)	Easy
35. Pinto Mountain	9.2 (14.8)	2850 (870)	3983 (1214)	Strenuous
36. Porcupine Wash and Ruby Lee Well	7.7 (12.4)	770 (235)	3081 (939)	Challenging
37. Mastodon Peak	2.8 (4.5)	500 (150)	3370 (1025)	Moderate
38. Lost Palms Oasis	7.2 (11.6)	1400 (425)	3446 (1050)	Challenging

VISITING JOSHUA TREE NATIONAL PARK

"Stabby plants and kitty litter." These were the colorful words a hiker used to describe the desert moments before I led a group of desert novices on an introductory hike in Joshua Tree National Park. A few of these hikers had ventured out reluctantly, carrying the burden of preconceived notions about what they would find: a hot, scorched wasteland that wanted nothing more than to hurt them in creative ways. The irony of the hiker's statement hit home moments later when I led the group into a lush oasis of California fan palms nourished by permanent water sources. We discussed how the desert's oases harbor a diverse array of wildlife, like seaports on the edge of the Pacific, and how the indigenous peoples from ages long gone cultivated and nourished the oases while benefiting from their abundant resources. In the midst of all that kitty litter, we found a vibrant secret that ultimately turned the desert skeptic into a desert enthusiast.

No portion of the vast Southern California deserts epitomizes the joy of discovering the desert's surprising beauty quite as well as Joshua Tree National Park. It is true that you will find an appropriate amount of plants that could stab, poke, prick, rake, snag, and swat you. And yes, many of the park's washes and trails feature sand that fills the fever dreams of felines everywhere. However, spend only a scant amount

OPPOSITE *Gardens of pinnacles in the Jumbo Rocks area*

of time within this sprawling desert park and you will become enamored with the famous monzogranite boulder piles, evocative Joshua tree woodlands, windswept mountain peaks and ridges, a colorful and sometimes sordid history spanning centuries, rugged canyons and sinuous washes lined with a diverse mixture of geology and vegetation, seemingly infinite open space, the aforementioned palm oases, and sublime solitude for those who know where to look.

Joshua Tree's 790,636 acres encompass an area slightly larger than the state of Rhode Island. The park boundaries overlap two separate deserts, the Mojave and the Colorado, with the higher, cooler Mojave Desert comprising the western half of the park and the lower, hotter Colorado Desert comprising the eastern half. A transition zone running along the bases of the Hexie and Pinto Mountains marks the boundary between the two deserts and contains botanical features of both. The extreme western quarter of the park includes the Little San Bernardino Mountains, a rugged region of peaks, ridges, valleys, and canyons whose higher elevations and slightly closer proximity to cooler coastal temperatures produce habitats that are somewhere between conifer-draped mountains and arid desert valleys. In stark contrast, the vast expanse of Pinto Basin, ringed by the arid Pinto, Coxcomb, Eagle, Cottonwood, and Hexie Mountains, dominates the park's eastern half.

The park's main thoroughfare, Park Boulevard, runs west to east from the park's West Entrance Station, which is south of the Joshua Tree Visitor Center in the town of Joshua Tree. As it crosses the park, it passes through a series of valleys, including Lost Horse Valley, Hidden Valley, and Queen Valley, before connecting with Pinto Basin Road just south of the park's North Entrance Station and headquarters in Twenty-nine Palms. Aside from a relatively small strip of land on either side of the aforementioned roads, the remainder of Joshua Tree's acreage is designated wilderness. These valleys

A pot of monzogranite at the end of every rainbow

contain the park's signature features: beautifully sculpted monzogranite rock piles and the Joshua tree. Although these valleys comprise a much smaller part of the park than you may expect, here you will find the majority of the hiking trails and park highlights, three of the park's most popular campgrounds, most of its picnic areas, nearly all of its rock-climbing destinations, and its most celebrated scenery.

Pinto Basin Road splits from Park Boulevard at Pinto Wye, just south of Twentynine Palms, and heads southwest through the dramatic transition between the Mojave and Colorado Deserts. In stark contrast to the high valleys of the Mojave, the Colorado Desert is a different world altogether, with sun-blasted mountain ranges bounding the sprawling expanse of Pinto Basin. After threading its way through Pinto Basin, Pinto Basin Road reaches the Cottonwood Visitor Center, where you will find the bulk of the facilities serving Joshua Tree's eastern half. Pinto Basin Road then passes the park's southern boundary on its way to the busy asphalt artery of Interstate 10.

HUMAN HISTORY

Human history in the area now known as Joshua Tree National Park follows a pattern typical to many other places in Southern California: millennia of indigenous habitation followed by Spanish exploration, displacement of Native peoples, and European American settlement with the intention of exploiting the area's resources. Like many other public parks, Joshua Tree's establishment followed years of conservation activism to establish political protection of the area as a national monument, which later led to further legislative action to establish the national park.

INDIGENOUS PEOPLES

Historians regard the Pinto people as the first inhabitants of this region. They lived in and around the area known as Pinto Basin around nine thousand years ago during a period when the climate was much cooler and wetter. The favorable climate supported a dramatically different habitat than today's arid desert, but as the climate warmed and dried out, the Pinto people vanished. Later tribes, including the Cahuilla in the south and the Serrano and Chemehuevi in the north, inhabited areas where permanent water sources enabled survival in the otherwise inhospitable landscape. Although Joshua Tree's flora can seem downright hostile at times, the area's indigenous peoples were masters at using nearly every local plant for food and medicine.

EUROPEANS ARRIVE

Pedro Fages, a Spanish explorer, first happened upon the area during a manhunt that originated in today's San Diego County. Other settlers and explorers passed through the region soon thereafter. However, it wasn't until European Americans discovered Joshua Tree's hitherto unknown resources that the mass displacement of Native peoples accelerated in favor of cattle ranching and mining. Cattle

Two-bedroom cabin available: some renovation required

preferred the abundant bunchgrasses of the high valleys, and
cattlemen left their mark on the landscape by constructing
"tanks," which are essentially small reservoirs, to catch run-
off and form a semipermanent water supply for their herds.
Barker Dam is the most famous example of these tanks.

RESOURCE EXPLOITATION

Not long after the discovery of Joshua Tree's suitability as
rangeland, miners set claims in what would later become
Lost Horse Valley and Queen Valley. Soon after, new claims,
gold mines, and their boomtowns began sprouting throughout the landscape like mushrooms after a spring rainstorm.
Few of these mines ever produced much in the way of
bullion—the Lost Horse Mine is one notable exception—but
the presence of so many miners altered the landscape in
numerous ways. Abandoned mine shafts and prospects pepper the area's mountain ranges, and much of the litter of that
era still lies scattered about for curious modern explorers to
discover. Many of the names of significant people from the

More precious than gold: water in the desert

mining era, such as Johnny Lang, William Keys, and J. D. Ryan, adorn landforms throughout the park. Bits and pieces of their legacies remain interwoven into the landscape and the hiking routes that cross it.

CONSERVATION AND THE ESTABLISHMENT OF THE PARK

As grazing and mining activity continued to leave unsightly scars on the landscape, conservation-minded individuals who had developed a deep attachment to the high-desert wonderlands began organizing toward political protection.

Of those conservationists, the figure of Minerva Hoyt looms largest over Joshua Tree. The former Southern belle turned president of the International Deserts Conservation League lobbied the Franklin D. Roosevelt administration for federal protection of the high-desert valleys, Joshua trees, and boulder piles of the Little San Bernardino Mountains. After years of lobbying spearheaded by Hoyt, President Roosevelt signed the executive order designating Joshua Tree National Monument in 1936.

Joshua Tree remained a monument for the next fifty-eight years until President Bill Clinton signed the California Desert Protection Act, which elevated the monument to national park status. The act also added significant acreage within the low-desert basins and ranges in the eastern half of the park, further increasing the diversity protected within park borders. Today's national park sees 1.5 to 2.5 million visitors annually, with hikers, campers, climbers, and sightseers permanently replacing the dusty old miners and cattle rustlers.

FLORA AND FAUNA

For a landscape that appears desolate at first glance, Joshua Tree National Park features a surprising range of biodiversity in both its flora and fauna. The park straddles two distinct desert regions, the Mojave and Colorado Deserts, both of which support distinct floral schemes.

Hundreds of different species call Joshua Tree home, including 52 mammal species, 44 reptile species,

A sun-worshipping chuckwalla

A Joshua tree salutes the sun as the storm passes.

more than 250 bird species, 75 species of butterflies, count-less insects, and even 2 species of amphibians.

Most species in the desert are nocturnal, with only birds, a few lizards, the occasional jackrabbit, and ground squirrels braving the midday heat. With water sources being scarce, most animals here either use water more efficiently than their relatives in wetter climates, or they have adaptations that allow them to survive on water that they obtain from eating plants or prey.

THE JOSHUA TREE

No other floral species in Joshua Tree National Park invites as much wonder, curiosity, and reverence as its namesake species, the Joshua tree (*Yucca brevifolia*). They thrive in open desert grasslands such as Lost Horse Valley and Queen Valley, as well as along the slopes and valleys of the Little San Bernardino Mountains in the western half of the park. Although technically not a tree, these yuccas assume a tree-like form that contorts into shapes evoking penance, prayer, and torture. Joshua trees lack tree rings, which makes it difficult to gauge their precise ages. However, biologists generally accept that Joshua trees can live longer than five hundred years, with the oldest believed to have lived for nearly one thousand years.

Legend has it that the Joshua tree received its common name from Mormon pioneers crossing the vast valleys of the Mojave. The tree's outstretched branches reportedly reminded the Mormons of the Biblical figure Joshua with his arms outstretched to the heavens in prayer. Modern-day visitors may find that the tree reminds them of the Truffula trees from Dr. Seuss's *The Lorax*. Not all historical figures were impressed, however. John C. Frémont, an early American explorer, described it as "the most repulsive tree in the vegetable kingdom." I'm guessing John C. Grump-a-Saurus never spent an afternoon wandering Lost Horse Valley as the evening light cast the trees in striking silhouettes. The rock band U2 had a different response. The tree inspired their biggest commercial and artistic success, the 1987 album *The Joshua Tree*.

More than the Joshua tree's significance in historic and popular culture, its reproductive process inspired Charles Darwin so much that he called it "the most wonderful case of fertilisation ever published." The tree relies on a symbiotic relationship with the yucca moth, which collects pollen from the tree's flowers and disperses it to other nearby trees. In exchange, the moth lays its eggs in the flowers, and the caterpillars eat some of the seeds in a mutually beneficial trade of pollination for sustenance.

Top row: California barrel cactus and blossom; bottom row: ocotillo and blossom

CACTI AND DESERT SCRUB

Beyond the Joshua tree, one of the first images that comes to mind when people consider the desert is that of the cactus. Visitors might therefore be surprised to find that cacti are something of a minority in Joshua Tree's Mojave Desert vegetation schema. The high valleys contain a few suitably wicked-looking species, such as silver cholla and pencil cholla. Benign cacti with gorgeous, showy flowers also grace rocky outcrops and unobtrusive patches of sand in open desert. Most notably, the brilliant red blossoms of the Mojave mound cactus and the flamboyant pink blossoms of the beavertail cactus will impress visitors in April.

Silver cholla catching the light

The cacti species come into their element when you transition into the lower, hotter Colorado Desert. Most of the Southwest's cactus species reside within the Sonoran Desert, of which California's Colorado Desert is only a small subunit. Within the Mojave-Colorado transition zone and deep into the Colorado Desert itself, you will find the wicked, ironically named teddy bear cholla, California barrel cactus, matted cholla, and hedgehog cactus. In addition to the cacti, you'll encounter the Colorado Desert's hallmark species, the ocotillo, a shrub with candelabra-like limbs coated in rigid spines. The ocotillo leafs out following storms, and it produces bright crimson flowers during spring.

KING CREOSOTE

Creosote, one of the most ubiquitous desert species, grows in the basins, valleys, and bajadas of both the low desert and the Mojave. Creosote may not seem like the most exciting plant, but visit during and immediately after a rainstorm, and its sweet, pervasive aroma will convince you otherwise. Fun fact about creosote: these plants can (but don't always) reproduce by cloning. The shrubs on the desert floor come and go, but the root system can survive for thousands of years. Biologists estimate that the King Clone creosote in nearby Lucerne Valley is about 11,700 years old, making it one of the older living organisms on the planet.

PINYON-JUNIPER WOODLAND

Cacti aside, you are likely to find large California junipers with fragrant, scaly needles and light-blue seed cones; bunchgrasses; and a variety of flowering shrubs throughout the valleys. Pinyon pines, Muller oaks, manzanita, and an assortment of other yucca species, including Mojave yucca and nolina, are common around the monzogranite rock piles north of Lost Horse and Queen Valleys. These thirstier species thrive on pockets of moisture and soil held within deep creases in the rocks. Mountain slopes host a sparser mix of all of these species in open plant communities.

THE CALIFORNIA FAN PALM

Finally, no cursory examination of the park's flora is complete without mentioning the California fan palm. Joshua

CLIMATE CHANGE IN THE PARK

In the last several decades, the overall trend in Southern California's climate can be summed up in two words: hotter and drier. With some notably wet years excepted, average rainfall totals continue to decline while average temperatures get a little warmer every year. This combination of heat and drought has the potential to dramatically reduce the habitat of the Joshua tree, as well as many of the other high-desert specimens. When climates warm, usually over the span of thousands of years, plant communities tend to migrate upward. At Joshua Tree, there isn't a lot of "up" for the plants to travel toward. If present trends continue, climatologists expect that only 10 percent of the park's current population density of Joshua trees will remain by the year 2100.

The juniper and the monolith near Jumbo Rocks Campground

Tree contains a handful of palm oases, the most notable of which are at Lost Palms Oasis and Fortynine Palms Oasis. Although many people associate Southern California with palms, the iconic trees found throughout Los Angeles, Santa Barbara, and San Diego are imported exotics from Mexico, the Canary Islands, and other tropical locales. The palms you see in Joshua Tree are the state's only native palm species. It may come as a mystery that a tropical species could thrive in one of the hottest and driest places on the planet. The answer to this botanical riddle is the presence of perennial springs created by the numerous faults in the area. Subterranean water percolates up through cracks created by the faults, and when it reaches the surface or just below the surface, it provides the palms—as well as numerous mammals, birds, reptiles, and amphibians—with the water that they need.

WILDFLOWERS

Joshua Tree's vast valleys and mountain slopes also host annual wildflower blooms. Some of these blooms, most notably the showy cacti blossoms, come from perennial plants. However, many of the best blooms erupt courtesy of desert annuals. Because annual flowers require just the right set of circumstances to bloom in profusion, a so-called super bloom—wherein massive fields of flowers bloom in unison—is a rare and ephemeral event. California's deserts can go years with only sparse blooms, until one of those rare rainy winters soaks the landscape. When this happens, the billions of seeds that lie dormant in the desert sand germinate all at once, transforming the park into a honey-scented flower garden.

Clockwise from upper left: Mojave aster, chia, desert chicory, hedgehog cactus, and desert blue bells

SUPER BLOOMS

Catching a super bloom is a matter of luck and timing. While there are flowers every spring following even the driest of winters, the true super blooms tend to occur only after winters where the deserts receive 125–200 percent of their average annual rainfall. March is prime time for wildflowers in the low deserts below 3000 feet (900 m). At elevations above 4000 feet (1200 m), blooms tend to happen in early April.

If you want to catch a super bloom, you can check with the park periodically throughout the rainy season to get a sense of what kind of winter they're having. You can also check with the park during the spring to get intel about the flowers. If there's a truly memorable bloom in the works, there's also a good chance that the event will be blasted all over traditional and social media.

BIGHORN SHEEP

Joshua Tree contains between two hundred and three hundred desert bighorn sheep, which are a subspecies in a larger population of bighorns that range throughout the Southern California and Baja California deserts and mountains. Bighorns are active at night, which is why you're likely to find day-use restrictions at popular areas like the Wonderland of Rocks. These large mammals prefer rocky terrain, and their agility allows them to scale difficult slopes with an ease that is the envy of the rock-climbing community. Of the three herds in the park (Eagle Mountains, Little San Bernardino Mountains, and the Wonderland of Rocks), the smallest herd, in the Wonderland of Rocks, is the one most visitors witness. This

Hi! How are ewe?

group frequents the Barker Dam area after dawn when they come to tank up on water before bedding down for the day.

RATTLESNAKES

Much to the concern of wary hikers, the park contains seven different species of rattlesnake, and each one prefers slightly different terrain. Rattlesnakes are extremely interested in avoiding humans, and although their rattles have a primal effect on hikers, the function of the rattle is to alert you to back off and give it space. Rattlesnakes generally attack only when they have no other option, and that usually happens only when humans corner them or try to handle them. Keep your eyes peeled as you walk, and especially watch where you put your hands when you're scrambling. If you spot them in advance, they won't pose a threat and will only add a bit of spice to your experience.

MOUNTAIN LIONS

Hikers should also note that mountain lions are present and active in the park. Although they have a fearsome reputation, they are seldom seen and prefer to avoid humans in much the same way that skittish house cats avoid guests. Like most animals in the park, they are active from dusk to dawn, so your chances of seeing them are greatest if you're an early bird or a sunset chaser. If you do encounter a mountain lion, do not run. Running triggers a predatory response. Stand your ground, and make yourself appear as large as possible. Make a lot of noise to signal that you're not food. If possible, slowly back away until you put a healthy amount of distance between yourself and the cat. Fight back if it attacks.

GEOLOGY: A WONDERLAND OF ROCKS

Taking center stage alongside the Joshua tree, the park's rock formations dominate the scenery while enticing visitors to hike through, scramble upon, or climb them. These rock piles come to you courtesy of the White Tank monzo-granite formation, a vast body of granite that comprises the Wonderland of Rocks as well as the outcrops around Jumbo Rocks, Belle Campground, and White Tank Campground.

The park's granite formations originated deep under-ground when bubbles of magma percolated up toward, but never penetrated, the earth's surface. As these bubbles came to rest, they cooled inside vast chambers to eventually become what geologists call plutons of igneous (meaning formed from magma) rock. As the rock cooled and settled, a system of horizontal and diagonal joints and faults devel-oped. In some cases, plumes of magma were injected into these cracks and cooled at a different rate, creating veins of quartz that are apparent throughout the monzogranite areas. Subterranean water eroded the edges of these cracks and faults for millions of years in much the same way that a stream of running water rounds the edges of an ice cube. A combination of tectonic uplift and periodic flash floods, which washed away the overlying surface rock, exposed the boulder piles we see today.

THERE'S ANCIENT, AND THEN THERE'S ANCIENT

Although any rock in the park is incomprehensibly old by human standards, monzogranite is relatively young. Geolo-gists date the rocks back to about 100 million years ago. While that sounds impressive, consider that some gneiss formations in the park are up to 1.7 billion years old. That's a bit like a ninety-year-old adult hanging out next to a six-month-old infant.

A gneiss outcrop begs for a pun.

Within Joshua Tree National Park, the metamorphic rock known as gneiss (sounds like "nice") dominates the summits, ridges, and slopes of the Little San Bernardino Mountains, as well as many of the slopes of the Pinto and Hexie Mountains. The term "metamorphic" refers to a process where one type of rock is subjected to intense heat and pressure over a long period of time before transforming into something else. The gneiss in the park is ancient, with this particular rock dating back as far as 800 million to 1.7 billion years. Other metamorphic rocks, such as marble and quartzite, can be found in more remote mountainous sections.

SHAKE, RATTLE, AND ROLL

In concluding this description of Joshua Tree's geology, we have to mention Southern California's great elephant in the room, the San Andreas Fault. Many people outside of California know the fault as either the force that will one day turn Los Angeles into an island or the force that will one day level Southern California. However, the fault's contribution to the park's geography is far more dramatic and interesting than such misunderstandings. This fault represents a boundary where the Pacific Plate and the North American Plate are grinding past each other. The resulting tectonic collision has pushed up Joshua Tree's mountains as well as Southern California's towering ranges, including the Santa Rosa, San Jacinto, and San Bernardino Mountains. South of the park, the San Andreas is pulling the interior of south-central California apart like a starving man rips a leg from a roast chicken. This region, known as the Salton Trough, contains Southern California's lowest point at 227 feet below sea level.

If you visit Keys View on a clear day, the view can sweep the extent of this dramatic scene, including the shimmering blue Salton Sea to the southeast. Slowly scan the landscape from southeast to west, and you will take in the dusky, remote Santa Rosa Mountains leading into the rugged San

Jacintos and culminating at Mount San Jacinto's summit at 10,834 feet. Directly across from Mount San Jacinto, Mount San Gorgonio's often snowcapped alpine summit stands at 11,504 feet, Southern California's highest point.

MUST-SEE SIGHTS AND ACTIVITIES

The following list of activities and destinations represent the best of the best of what you can see and do at Joshua Tree National Park. Only some of these activities involve hiking, so be sure to set some of your time aside for these must-see highlights.

ROCK CLIMBING

In addition to being a world-class hiking destination, Joshua Tree also serves as a mecca for rock climbers. Spend any time around Hidden Valley and the Wonderland of Rocks, and you are certain to see climbers testing their skills on the park's famous monzogranite rock piles. Although discussion of rock-climbing techniques and destinations is beyond the scope of this volume, hikers interested in the activity can learn more by visiting the climbing section of the park's website www.nps.gov/jotr/planyourvisit/climbing.htm.

A climber takes a crack at Intersection Rock.

Additionally, the park permits numerous commercial rock-climbing outfitters to guide climbers of all experience levels on excursions.

KEYS RANCH

This former residence of Joshua Tree's biggest mining-era personality, William Keys, remains one of the best preserved historic structures in the park. The only way to access the ranch is by taking a ninety-minute tour guided by rangers that explores the grounds. Tickets are required and must be purchased in advance by calling 760-367-5522.

THE WONDERLAND OF ROCKS

Perhaps the most iconic of all of Joshua Tree's geologic wonders, this 12-square-mile maze of beautifully eroded monzogranite formations offers some of the best scenery and hiking in the park. Although much of the area is difficult to navigate, several hikes in this guide either skirt the margins or penetrate the heart of the Wonderland. Even if you

The cozy confines of Keys Ranch (photo by Joe Wimbrow)

Deep in the heart of the Wonderland of Rocks

have no plans to hike into the area, simply poking around the edges at places like Barker Dam or the Wall Street Mill will give you the quintessential Joshua Tree experience.

LOST HORSE MINE

Of the three hundred or so mines from Joshua Tree's colorful mining period, only the Lost Horse Mine managed to churn out anything close to a profit. Between 1894 and 1931, the operation produced 10,000 ounces of gold and 16,000 ounces of silver worth about $5 million in modern currency. Many of the mine's structures still stand, and even if the mine were nothing more than a few rusted tin cans and piles of tailings, its surrounding scenery is worth the 4.2-mile out-and-back hike. See Route 17 for further details.

KEYS VIEW

This popular viewpoint on the crest of the Little San Bernardino Mountains looks out across the Coachella Valley and beyond to some of Southern California's loftiest mountains. The elevation range between the Salton Sea to the southeast (-227 feet, -69 m) and the summit of Mount San Gorgonio to the west (11,503 feet, 3506 m) represents one of the widest elevation spreads anywhere in the country. Come here early

Voluptuous formations near Jumbo Rocks Campground

in the morning or just before sunset to see the entirety of this view bathed in dramatic golden-hour lighting.

GEOLOGY TOUR ROAD
Visitors who want to see some fascinating geology but don't want to set out on foot can follow this 18-mile (29 km) interpretive drive that runs through most of the length of Queen Valley. Passenger vehicles can make it for the first few miles, but the deeper you go, the more you will need a four-wheel-drive vehicle. Dog lovers who don't mind stepping aside for the occasional passing vehicle can also follow this route as one of the few dog-friendly footpaths in the park.

JUMBO ROCKS
This tourist hot spot, nestled in a large outcrop of monzogranite on the east end of Queen Valley, features the park's largest campground, several family-friendly trails, and some of the most iconic rock formations in the park. Start with appealing novelties like Split Rock, Skull Rock, and Face Rock, and extend your explorations to the many beautiful

formations scattered around the campground and the Split Rock picnic area to the north.

MOJAVE-COLORADO DESERT TRANSITION ZONE

The boundary between two major North American deserts—the Mojave and the Colorado—runs through the rough halfway point of Joshua Tree National Park. Plant species representative of each desert mingle in this narrow band of middle-elevation desert that marks the transition. The Cholla Cactus Garden's short nature trail is a great place to witness how the flora begins to change between the two zones. Just don't spend so much time staring at the scenery that you accidentally bump into the ironically named teddy bear cholla.

PINTO BASIN

This vast basin ringed with rugged mountain ranges comprises the bulk of Joshua Tree's eastern half. Although no true hiking trails penetrate the basin, hikers can simply wander about, perhaps even so far as the Pinto Basin sand dunes about a mile north from Turkey Flat. Come during the early morning or late evening to watch the low angle of the sun bathe the vast open space in golden light. A strenuous cross-country route leads to the high point of the Pinto Mountains, from which you can behold the vast basin in its entirety.

COTTONWOOD SPRING

The main hub of activity in the eastern half of the park, Cottonwood Spring features a pair of popular hiking routes. But perhaps more notable than the hiking, the spring features something exceptionally rare in the desert: shade. A reliable subterranean water source nourishes a dense grove of California fan palms and Fremont cottonwoods. Nearby bedrock mortars—circular depressions used to pulverize seeds and nuts—testify to the importance of this area to the Cahuilla people, who depended on the spring for water.

PLANNING YOUR TRIP

The success of any adventure in Joshua Tree National Park requires preparation, and within this section you will find all the information you'll need, including overviews on the park's visitor and nature centers, campgrounds, climate and weather, rules and regulations, and trail safety and etiquette.

VISITOR AND NATURE CENTERS

Joshua Tree National Park features four visitor centers from which you can purchase resources, view interpretive displays, obtain information about conditions in the park, talk to rangers and knowledgeable volunteers, and pick up souvenirs.

Black Rock Nature Center: Located at 9800 Black Rock Canyon Road, Yucca Valley, CA 92284 (within Black Rock Campground). Open daily from 8:00 AM to 4:00 PM (8:00 AM to 8:00 PM on Fridays), October through May. Phone: 760-367-3001.

Joshua Tree Visitor Center: Located at 6554 Park Boulevard, Joshua Tree, CA 92256 (north of the park's West Entrance Station and just south of State Route 62). Open daily from 8:00 AM to 5:00 PM. Phone: 760-366-1855.

Indian Cove Ranger Station: Located on Indian Cove Road, on the west side of Twentynine Palms and just north of Indian Cove Campground. Open daily from 8:00 AM to 5:00 PM. Phone: 760-367-5500.

OPPOSITE *Finding a way to keep cool on the Hidden Valley Trail (Route 12)*

Oasis Visitor Center and Park Headquarters: Located at 74485 National Park Drive, Twentynine Palms, CA 92277. Open daily from 8:30 AM to 5:00 PM. Phone: 760-367-5500.

Cottonwood Visitor Center: Located on Pinto Basin Road, Twentynine Palms, CA 92277. Open daily from 8:30 AM to 4:00 PM. Phone: 760-367-5500.

CAMPGROUNDS

Joshua Tree contains nine campgrounds, five of which are first come, first served, and four that accept reservations. Of the reservable campgrounds, Sheep Pass Group Campground is set aside exclusively for groups of more than 10. Numerous options for camping exist just outside the park, which is important since competition for campsites in the park during its peak season (spring) is fierce. You can save yourself a lot of trouble by attempting to reserve your campsite in advance, and park staff can direct you to dispersed camping options north and south of the park on Bureau of Land Management (BLM) property. Because campground fees are subject to change, contact the park ahead of time to verify the price.

One warning that I wish I didn't need to make: if you're thinking that you'd like to set up a hammock, abandon the idea now. The only options you'll have for stringing up a hammock are the surrounding Joshua trees. More and more Joshua trees topple every year because people attempt to string hammocks to them. They aren't strong enough to support the weight of human bodies.

Black Rock Campground is located at 9800 Black Rock Canyon Road, Yucca Valley, CA 92284, and it features 99 sites. With cell reception, trash/recycling pickup, an amphitheater, staff on-site, a dump station, potable water, flush toilets, nearby equestrian camping, and access to an expansive network of trails, Black Rock Campground has more amenities and creature comforts than the rest of the park's campgrounds. Routes 1 through 4 begin from within or adjacent to the campground, and the Black Rock Nature Center is a good place for information, resources, and souvenirs.

Hidden Valley Campground's popularity guarantees that its sites are almost always in high demand. Located on Park Boulevard, 10 miles (16 km) east of the West Entrance, this campground features 44 first-come, first-served sites tucked into the nooks and crannies at the base of some of the park's most popular climbing destinations.

Ryan Campground is another small but popular campground within Lost Horse Valley. It lies along Park Boulevard, 11 miles (18 km) east of the West Entrance, and contains 31 first-come, first-served sites adjacent to the Ryan Ranch Trail and Cap Rock Nature Trail.

Sheep Pass Group Campground offers campsites for groups of 10 to 60 people. Located atop Sheep Pass along Park Boulevard, 13.3 miles (21.4 km) east of the West Entrance, the campground has 6 reservable group sites.

Jumbo Rocks Campground is Joshua Tree's largest and most popular campground. It holds 124 sites, many of which are reservable between October and May. The campground is located on Park Boulevard, 17.3 miles (27.8 km) from the West Entrance and 8.1 miles (13 km) from the North Entrance. The Discovery Nature Trail and Skull Rock Nature Trail are easily accessible by foot from this campground.

Indian Cove Campground lies somewhat off the beaten path, 9 miles (14.5 km) east from the intersection of Park Boulevard and State Route 62, and 3.2 miles (5.1 km) south on Indian Cove Road. It contains 101 campsites, 13 of which are group sites; all sites are reservable from October to May.

Belle Campground is one of two small campgrounds located along Pinto Basin Road, 1.3 miles (2.1 km) south of Pinto Wye. It contains 18 first-come, first-served sites, which makes it one of the quieter campgrounds in the park.

Intimate details in the vastness of Pinto Basin at dawn

White Tank Campground is also along Pinto Basin Road, about 2.7 miles (4.3 km) south of Pinto Wye. It includes the Arch Rock Nature Trail. This campground holds 15 first-come, first-served sites.

Cottonwood Campground is the only campground in the eastern, low-desert side of the park, and it is located on Pinto Basin Road, 6.7 miles (10.8 km) north of Interstate 10. It contains 62 campsites, 3 of which are group sites, and reservations are available between October and May.

WHAT TO DO IF YOU GET SHUT OUT

During the busy season, camping at Joshua Tree can be a competitive contact sport, where only the ruthless emerge with a pitched tent and evening s'mores. While the best strategy for getting a spot remains planning way ahead and reserving a campsite, some people don't get that luxury for one reason or another. If you're taking a last-minute trip, and you learn from the rangers that every spot in the park is already occupied, you can take advantage of a large overflow camping area on BLM land north of the park at the intersection of Cascade and Sunflower Roads. Other possible overflow camping can be found on BLM land south of the park as well. Keep in mind that there are no facilities, including no fire rings, toilets, water, or trash collection at these dispersed camping areas. You will have to bring everything you need and pack it all out with you when you're done.

WHEN TO VISIT

Although you can visit Joshua Tree at any time throughout the year, the environmental factors that characterize the park's habitats make it a desirable place for physical exertion only during the cooler half of the year. Summertime in Joshua Tree can be a scorching affair, with temperatures routinely transcending triple digits (Fahrenheit) for days on end. You are far more likely to get good hiking conditions within the western high-desert portion of the park, which for the Southern California desert means temperatures below 85 degrees F (29° Celsius), between mid-October and mid-May.

For the low desert on the east side of the park, this window of good conditions is even shorter. You can expect prime conditions from early November to the end of March. Comfortable temperatures during October and April can be hit-or-miss at any elevation below 4000 feet (1200 m), so check the weather reports religiously if you plan to hike on the low-desert side.

CLIMATE AND WEATHER

As emphasized in the preceding section, weather is a major concern when it comes to visiting the park. Deserts can be exceptionally unfriendly places to human bodies, which store water inefficiently and struggle to regulate internal temperatures when things aren't just right. As if the extreme heat were not enough, you also have more unexpected factors such as extreme cold, extreme winds, extremely low humidity, and surprisingly, occasional snowfall above 4000 feet (1200 m).

Precipitation is a rare event in Joshua Tree. The higher Mojave side of the park receives an average of eight to ten inches annually, while the low desert averages around six inches annually. Deluges are rare, since the moisture-wringing barriers of the San Jacinto and San Bernardino Mountains steal most of the precipitation before incoming storms reach the park. This phenomenon, known as rain shadowing, creates the climatic conditions responsible for Joshua Tree's generally mild and sunny winters.

Although the bulk of the park's precipitation falls during California's winter, with somewhat less falling in autumn and spring, occasional summertime incursions of moist air from the Gulf of California can lead to conditions perfect for monsoonal thunderstorms. Thunderstorms are almost always isolated and localized in nature, but they can release prodigious amounts of precipitation in one spot. That much rain at once can produce flash flooding, during which massive walls of water career down normally dry canyons. Lightning and thunder accompany these atmospheric temper tantrums, so lightning strikes are a possible threat as well. If you see ominous, dark clouds building up nearby, leave canyons or washes immediately and retreat to the nearest shelter.

Mount San Gorgonio with its head in the clouds

All of these warnings aside, if you time your visit right, you will experience the sublime combination of mild temperatures, gentle breezes, and glorious sunshine for which Southern California residents shell out exorbitant sums of money to enjoy permanently.

PARK RULES AND REGULATIONS

In order to enter Joshua Tree National Park, you will have to pay a fee at one of the five main entrances. This includes the Black Rock Nature Center located within Black Rock Campground, the West Entrance Station south of the town of Joshua Tree, the Indian Cove Ranger Station north of Indian Cove Campground, the North Entrance Station south of Twentynine Palms, and the Cottonwood Visitor Center just north of the park's southern entrance. If you arrive when the fee kiosks are closed, you will be required to pay the fee on your way out. Entrance fees cover seven days, and you pay your fee only once, even if you enter, exit, and reenter the park at different entrance stations.

Exploring the Boy Scout Trail (Route 10)

Eighty-five percent of the park is designated wilderness, which protects the landscape in the most primitive form possible while excluding all mechanical transport (including bicycles) and tools. Trail and campground improvements are minimal in these areas, a good reminder to hikers to minimize their impact.

DAY-USE AREAS

Most of the trails included in this guide explore day-use areas designated to protect wildlife and curb overuse. The appropriate times to hike within day-use areas are between a half hour before sunrise and a half hour after sunset. Day-use areas are marked on the maps within this guide to give you a clearer picture of where these areas exist. The park's various picnic areas also fall within this same day-use designation and are subject to the same hours of operation.

BACKCOUNTRY CAMPING

Large parts of the park are open to public use, specifically backcountry camping, outside of daylight hours. The park utilizes a unique backcountry permit system wherein self-issue permits are available at thirteen separate backcountry registration boards. Unregistered cars are subject to citation and towing, and in some cases may trigger unnecessary search-and-rescue operations.

The park prohibits camping within 1 mile (1.6 km) of any road and requires that you also camp 500 feet (150 m) from the trail. Always select a durable surface to camp on, and pack out everything that you bring in, including used toilet paper, which takes a very long time to decompose in the desert and may ruin another hiker's experience. As for solid human waste, always bury it in cat holes at least six to eight inches deep. For more information on backpacking and backcountry permits, visit www.nps.gov/jotr/planyourvisit/backpacking.htm.

DOGS

As wonderful as it can be to have your best four-legged friend along with you, dogs are prohibited on all the routes within this guide. As with most national parks, dogs are allowed on paved and unpaved roads in Joshua Tree so long as they are leashed, and they are also welcome within campgrounds and picnic areas. If you find this restriction onerous, bear in mind that the park has deemed that pets pose a threat and disruption to wildlife, and given the park's mandate to protect the flora and fauna within it, wildlife gets priority.

FIREARMS

Federal law allows people who can legally possess firearms to carry them within the park provided they comply with state laws and regulations. Firearms are not permitted in certain facilities, and those facilities are always marked.

DRONES

Drones are remote-operated, unmanned aircraft that people often use for videography or for fun. However, to limit noise pollution, protect habitats, protect wildlife, and preserve scenic and wilderness values, the park forbids the use of drones. The only exception occurs when you have written permission from the park's superintendent.

CAMPFIRES

Campfires are permitted only within designated campfire rings. The desert is an extremely dry place, and extremely dry places also tend to be quite flammable. Over the last century, a number of invasive grasses and shrubs have established footholds in the park. These invasives tend to be flammable and can exacerbate wildfires. Joshua trees and other flora have few defenses against fire, and a careless human-caused conflagration can annihilate vast areas of habitat.

SAFETY

Despite Joshua Tree's outward appearance as a relatively benign playground full of striking rock formations and weird, twisted trees, it harbors a number of physical dangers that all hikers must be prepared for.

HEAT

Temperatures routinely hit triple digits during the summer, although uncomfortable temperatures (above 85 degrees Fahrenheit, 29° Celsius) may occur at any time of the year. Hiking in the heat can leave you dehydrated or suffering from heat cramps. At worst, heat cramps and dehydration can evolve into heat exhaustion and then heatstroke. Heatstroke, if left unchecked, can rapidly result in death. In the most basic terms, heat-related injuries involve the body losing its ability to internally regulate temperatures, which essentially cooks your internal organs. Your single best strategy for avoiding heat-related injuries is to avoid hiking in the heat. Check the forecast religiously before your visit for temperatures rising above 80 degrees F (27° C), and stay off the trails during the hottest parts of the day (10:00 AM to 4:00 PM).

ARIDITY

The park's lack of permanent water sources is of particular concern to backpackers, but dryness can impact hikers even on short and moderate day hikes. The low relative humidity that the desert is famous for can dry out human beings who lack the evolved defense mechanisms of desert flora and fauna to cope with dry conditions. Carry and consume liberal amounts of water. Two liters per person for a 5-mile hike is good, but four liters is always better. It's better to carry a heavy pack and be able to drink liberally than to run out of water on a hot day.

SUN EXPOSURE

Nearly every hike in Joshua Tree lacks shade, leaving hikers open to the cruel, punishing desert sun. Carry adequate sun protection in the form of sunscreen, and reapply it about every two hours. A wide-brim hat can keep the sun off your face and neck, and sunglasses block UV rays from scorching your sensitive retinas. Light-colored, loose-

Teddy bear cholla are not good for cuddling.

fitting clothes help to reflect some of the sunshine, whereas dark-colored clothing absorbs heat. Hikers may even consider carrying a reflective umbrella to block the worst of the sun's fury on long, exposed hikes.

COLD

Much of Joshua Tree's high-desert region sits between 3500 and 5800 feet (1050 and 1770 m). When cold Pacific storms sweep through the region, they may bring nighttime temperatures into the 30s and even 20s (Fahrenheit)—a nasty shock for visitors expecting heat. Even daytime temperatures can linger in the 40s during these times. Dressing in layers is the best way to handle cold temperatures, as opposed to wearing a single large, bulky jacket. Being able to add or subtract layers as you go allows you more flexibility to cope with temperature fluctuations.

STABBY PLANTS

Many of the desert's plants have evolved defenses to ward off both the heat and the possibility of being consumed by animals. Chief among those defenses are cactus spines, which turn innocent plants into medieval torture devices. Cholla cacti are perhaps the cruelest as their spines have tiny hooks that embed deep into your skin and resist your efforts to pull them out. As if that were not enough, you also get to dodge sharp, brittle yucca leaves, catclaw acacia, mesquite, and ocotillo that scratch, grab, and gouge. Your best strategy to avoid becoming a pincushion is to step lightly and carefully. Losing concentration on what you are doing, especially during off-trail travel, is an invitation to test out your first-aid kit.

TREACHEROUS TERRAIN

The beautiful rock piles of Joshua Tree practically beg you to climb them. Enticing though they are, they remain uneven surfaces with steep drops and numerous hazards. Other parts of the park feature jagged rock underfoot, steep slopes, and narrow canyons. Successful navigation of this kind of terrain requires caution and patience as well as sturdy hiking boots with good tread. An even better rule of thumb for people less inclined to take chances is to stick to the trails whenever possible.

CROSS-COUNTRY TRAVEL

Although most of the trails in Joshua Tree are clearly marked and easy to follow, this guide does contain some cross-country routes that veer away from established paths. In these instances, it is crucial that you possess a high-quality map, preferably a USGS topographic map featuring fine topographic detail, a compass, and the ability to use both. Hikers have become lost in the park with fatal consequences, especially in places like the Maze and the Wonderland of Rocks. If you doubt your navigational

Oh, just another mind-blowing Pinto Basin sunrise—no biggie.

ability, avoid the routes featuring cross-country travel and stick to the established trails. Do not rely on GPS tracks or cell phones for navigation, as both devices are known to fail.

DANGER NOODLES

Despite their fierce reputation, rattlesnakes (a.k.a. danger noodles) are rather shy and retiring, and they will avoid you at all costs. They become dangerous when they are no longer able to avoid you, which usually happens when hikers inadvertently get too close. This is particularly likely around rock piles in which rattlesnakes curl up and hide in the crevices. Always watch where you are stepping or placing your hands.

MOUNTAIN LIONS

Mountain lions are a large apex predator that primarily hunt deer and bighorn sheep. They are shy, reclusive, and mostly nocturnal. This means that most hikers will never see one. Hikers who set out before dawn or continue past dusk have a slightly higher chance of encountering them. If you do meet a mountain lion, confront it face-to-face and make a ton of noise. Appear as large as possible and do not run. Fleeing may trigger a predatory response that convinces the cat that you're a meal. If attacked, fight back. Report any sightings or incidents with mountain lions to the rangers immediately.

THE TEN ESSENTIALS

The point of the Ten Essentials, originated by the Mountaineers, has always been to answer two basic questions: Can you prevent emergencies and respond positively should one occur (items 1–5)? And can you safely spend a night—or more—outside (items 6–10)? Use this list as a guide and tailor it to the needs of your outing.

1. **Navigation:** The five fundamentals are a map, altimeter, compass, GPS device, and a personal locator beacon or other device to contact emergency first responders.
2. **Headlamp:** Include spare batteries.
3. **Sun protection:** Wear sunglasses, sun-protective clothes, and broad-spectrum sunscreen rated at least SPF 30.
4. **First aid:** Basics include bandages; skin closures; gauze pads and dressings; roller bandage or wrap; tape; antiseptic; blister prevention and treatment supplies; nitrile gloves; tweezers; needle; nonprescription painkillers; anti-inflammatory, anti-diarrheal, and antihistamine tablets; topical antibiotic; and any important personal prescriptions, including an EpiPen if you are allergic to bee or hornet venom.
5. **Knife:** Also consider a multitool, strong tape, some cordage, and gear repair supplies.
6. **Fire:** Carry at least one butane lighter (or waterproof matches) and firestarter, such as chemical heat tabs, cotton balls soaked in petroleum jelly, or commercially prepared firestarter.
7. **Shelter:** In addition to a rain shell, carry a single-use bivy sack, plastic tube tent, or jumbo plastic trash bag.
8. **Extra food:** For shorter trips a one-day supply is reasonable.
9. **Extra water:** Carry sufficient water and have the skills and tools required to obtain and purify additional water.

10. **Extra clothes:** Pack additional layers needed to survive the night in the worst conditions that your party may realistically encounter.

LEAVE NO TRACE

In any place this popular, it is imperative that hikers adhere to Leave No Trace principles. Although LNT principles don't always have the weight of the law behind them, following these guidelines is imperative because your caution and care helps mitigate overuse so that everybody else can enjoy the park as much as you do. You may have noticed that I already touched on some of these principles elsewhere as part of park regulations, but when it comes to hiking responsibly, the principles involved merit repetition.

PLAN AHEAD AND PREPARE

Nothing guarantees success in life as much as preparation, and that same principle carries through to hiking. Many hikers get into trouble because they run into conditions they did not prepare for; a lot of difficulties hikers encounter are wholly avoidable. You can avoid similar hardships by knowing the regulations and concerns of the park, monitoring weather conditions, traveling outside of the times of highest use, visiting in small groups when possible, and using a map and compass to ensure you don't have to make additions like cairns or ribbons to find your way.

TRAVEL AND CAMP ON DURABLE SURFACES

Although Joshua Tree National Park has specific rules about the distance your backcountry campsite must be from roads and trails, they also expect that you will camp on durable surfaces free of vegetation. Although many of the routes in this guide follow formal trails, a substantial fraction go off-trail through washes and occasionally along ridges and open desert. In these instances, it's best to tread lightly by endeavoring not to trample vegetation or by sticking to informal paths wherever they exist.

DISPOSE OF WASTE PROPERLY

Please put all trash and other refuse into the appropriate receptacle. Joshua Tree provides trash receptacles at nearly all formal trailheads. You are responsible for carrying out everything you bring in with you. The one exception here is poop, which you should bury in a six-to-eight-inch-deep cat hole. Pack out your toilet paper in a plastic bag. It takes a long time for toilet paper to biodegrade in dry climates, and animals will dig the paper up and scatter it around the landscape.

MINIMIZE CAMPFIRE IMPACTS

Given how dry this environment is, you can have a fire only in an approved container. Try to keep your fire small so that sparks don't drift off into dry brush. Make sure your fire is dead out, and scatter the ashes around to allow them to cool thoroughly.

RESPECT WILDLIFE

Respecting wildlife is actually a formal law at Joshua Tree. You are not supposed to handle or bother wildlife in any way, and you should attempt to keep at least ten feet between yourself and any wild animal you encounter. Feeding such creatures alters their behaviors and can make them aggressive. It can lead to injuries, and in some cases, it can force the park to euthanize the aggressive animal.

BE CONSIDERATE OF OTHER VISITORS

A good rule of thumb here is to remember that every person you cross paths with on the trail spent a lot of time, money, and effort to get to the same place. They are all trying to enjoy their trip, and therefore you should extend whatever courtesy is reasonably within your power to ensure that you don't wreck someone else's experience. Specifically, this principle asks that you yield to others on the trail to reduce conflict and let the sounds of nature prevail. This includes not playing music out loud through your phone or your Bluetooth speakers. Not everybody wants to hear music on the trail, and out of respect, it's best that you use headphones if you want to rock out.

SUGGESTED ITINERARIES

The two itineraries presented here assume that you are traveling west to east along Park Boulevard from the West Entrance, south of the town of Joshua Tree, and out the Cottonwood Spring exit, at the southeast corner of the park.

ONE DAY

This itinerary stops at a handful of short interpretive trails that bestow a bit of geologic and natural history knowledge while visiting some of the park's most memorable sites. You will also enjoy a tour of historic Keys Ranch while taking in expansive views across the Coachella Valley from Keys View.

- Keys Ranch: A ninety-minute guided tour takes you through the former residence of mining-era personality William Keys.
- Barker Dam (Route 13): A short looping hike around a man-made reservoir.
- Keys View (best at sunset): Sweeping views span the Coachella Valley and surrounding mountain ranges.
- Skull Rock Nature Trail (Route 26): A popular loop hike visiting several peculiar rock formations.
- Cholla Cactus Garden (Route 34): Look but don't touch on this introduction to the desert's most sinister denizen.

- Cottonwood Spring: Visit a shady watering hole with native features. Include the Mastodon Peak hike (Route 37) if time permits.

THREE DAYS

This three-day itinerary incorporates three memorable, moderate half-day hikes followed by shorter routes and other non-hiking destinations. This itinerary takes you to some of the most popular features in the park as well as some of its most notable hikes.

Day One:
- Willow Hole (Route 11): An excursion deep into the Wonderland of Rocks.
- Keys Ranch: A ninety-minute guided tour takes you through the former residence of mining-era personality William Keys.
- Barker Dam (Route 13): A short looping hike around a man-made reservoir.
- Keys View (best at sunset): Sweeping views span the Coachella Valley and surrounding mountain ranges.

Day Two:
- Lost Horse Mine (Route 17): Take a satisfying loop hike that visits Joshua Tree's largest, once most profitable mine.
- Skull Rock Nature Trail (Route 26): A popular loop hike visiting several peculiar rock formations.
- Fortynine Palms Oasis (Route 31): Take a moderate hike to a lush palm grove nourished by springs.

Day Three:
- Arch Rock Nature Trail (Route 33): Enjoy an easy hike to a rock arch within White Tank Campground.
- Cholla Cactus Garden (Route 34): Look but don't touch on this introduction to the desert's most sinister denizen.

KEY STATS: JOSHUA TREE NATIONAL PARK

- Date established: October 31, 1994 (it became a national monument in 1936)
- Acreage: 790,636 acres
- Area designated as wilderness: More than 54 percent
- Low point: 934 feet (285 m, Pinto Wells)
- High point: 5813 feet (1772 m, Quail Mountain)
- Average annual visitation: 1.5 to 2.5 million
- Height of tallest Joshua Tree in the park: 40 feet (12 m, Queen Valley)
- First group of humans known to inhabit area: Pinto Culture

- Lost Palms Oasis (Route 38) and Cottonwood Spring: Visit the park's largest grove of California fan palms by hiking out to Lost Palms Oasis, or just enjoy the shade and native features at Cottonwood Spring, where the Lost Palms Oasis route starts.

Desert hiking always carries a measure of risk, but the considerations covered in this chapter arm you with the knowledge you need to minimize your risk. With a healthy respect for the desert's specific challenges and hazards, and with good judgment and preparation, you are now ready to enjoy Southern California's premier desert wonderland.

HOW TO USE THIS GUIDE

This book contains an assortment of hikes catering to everyone from toddlers taking their first steps to dedicated desert rats looking for a challenge. These hikes showcase the park's natural, historical, and geologic variety and represent a sample of every aspect of Joshua Tree, including its diverse range of flora, alluring boulder piles, colorful human history, soaring vistas, and stunning open spaces.

Here you'll find short nature trails, casual hikes to historical sites, moderate summit ascents, rambling explorations of fantastic geologic features, satisfying half-day hikes that sample a variety of highlights, and a few challenging cross-country hikes to notable park high points that can double as overnight routes. In short, these curated hikes represent the best of what Joshua Tree has to offer. This by no means includes every possible route that Joshua Tree contains, but it's enough to keep even the biggest fan of the park busy for a long time.

GEOGRAPHIC REGIONS

This guide breaks down the park into six geographic regions arranged from the northwest end of the park to the southeast end of the park. The first four chapters cover the high-desert areas.

OPPOSITE *A Tetris game frozen in time*

Black Rock Canyon consists of the trail network accessible from Black Rock Campground, and each route visits a view-packed high point.

The **West Entrance** section encompasses the geographic region between the park's West Entrance Station south of the Joshua Tree Visitor Center and Hidden Valley. Much of this terrain is rugged and lightly visited, and it provides options for hikers looking for more extensive explorations.

Lost Horse Valley contains many of the park's most notable highlights, as well as its most popular hiking trails.

Queen Valley also features a number of popular routes centered around Jumbo Rocks Campground and the various mining claims on the northeast end of the valley.

The last two chapters cover lower elevation desert along the northern boundary of the park and surrounding Pinto Basin in the east. **Indian Cove and the North Entrance** refers to the geographic region south of Twentynine Palms, which includes several trailheads dispersed along State Route 62, Park Boulevard, and Pinto Basin Road.

Pinto Basin and Cottonwood Spring contains a mix of cross-country routes and popular trails that survey the spectrum of low-desert highlights.

KEY HIKE INFORMATION

Each hike begins with the following information to help you get a good handle on key characteristics of the route.

DISTANCE, ELEVATION GAIN, AND HIGH POINT

These categories refer to the distance a hike covers, the amount of elevation gain, and the high point for the route. Note that this guide displays cumulative elevation gain, as opposed to calculating the difference between the lowest and highest points on a hike. This gives hikers a better handle on how much climbing is in store. All values are listed in both the US standard (English) and metric systems.

A standout specimen above Black Rock Canyon

All distances, elevation gain, and high points were derived from GPS data collected during field work and extrapolated through CalTopo.com. Please note that due to the inherent variability of GPS data, your mileage may vary slightly from what's presented here. All elevations except for high points are rounded to the nearest five.

DIFFICULTY AND TRAIL SURFACE

Each hike is categorized into one of four separate ratings for difficulty: easy, moderate, challenging, and strenuous. These ratings are calibrated toward the mythical "average hiker" who maintains a reasonable degree of fitness and has at least some desert hiking experience. Bear in mind that many hikers fall on either side of average. Please understand that your fitness level and experience may skew these ratings.

Easy: Short, family-friendly hikes that nearly all hikers can finish comfortably. Approximately 0.4 mile to 3 miles (0.6 to 4.8 km) and up to 300 feet (90 m) of elevation gain.

Moderate: Longer hikes that most reasonably fit hikers can complete in two to four hours. Approximately 2.5–7 miles (4–11 km) and up to 850 feet (260 m) of elevation gain.

Challenging: Half-day hikes suitable for experienced hikers that may also contain some cross-country navigation, difficult terrain, and steep slopes. Approximately 2–9 miles (3–14.5 km) and up to 1500 feet (455 m) of elevation gain.

Strenuous: Full-day hikes suitable for experienced, well-conditioned hikers that contain cross-country navigation, difficult terrain, and steep slopes. Approximately 8–11 miles (13–18 km) and up to 3000 feet (915 m) of elevation gain.

Although difficulty typically relates to the length of a hike and the amount of climbing involved, factors such as terrain, steep slopes, cross-country navigation, and other obstacles may affect the ratings. Conditions on trails vary dramatically throughout Joshua Tree, and that information is covered in the trail surface section.

MAPS

The appropriate USGS topographic map to refer to for routefinding is listed in the maps section. Given the nature of desert travel, which often includes travel on unnamed washes, confusing terrain, and occasionally a complete lack of formal trail, it is *highly recommended* that hikers use a topographic map and a compass on routes that call for routefinding. Other maps such as those published by National Geographic make good reference sources, but

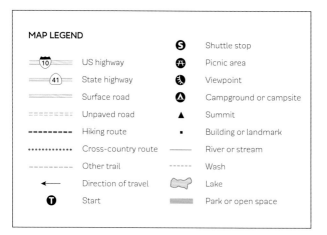

they often present trails in a misleading fashion. Additionally, their topographic data is too small and cramped to be a useful aid in routefinding.

USGS topos are the most reliable source of topographic information. You can purchase them directly from the USGS website: www.usgs.gov/products/maps/topo-maps. In addition, the website CalTopo.com is a phenomenal online resource that, among many other things, allows you to customize topographic maps specifically for the hike you wish to take.

GPS COORDINATES

This section provides GPS coordinates for the location of each trailhead. Coordinates are listed in decimal degrees (based on the WGS84 datum), as that's the easiest way to enter the coordinates into many websites and applications like Google Maps.

NOTES

The notes section includes specific information related to terrain, navigation, whether a hike is open to day use or overnight use, whether there's a restroom or toilet at the trailhead, whether the trail has interpretive features, or any other unique quality that merits mention.

HIKE DESCRIPTIONS

Beyond the key hike information, each hike has three or four sections: a paragraph describing the hike's notable features, specific challenges, and other unique features; driving directions; a detailed mile-by-mile account of the hike itself; and an optional going farther section that covers ways to extend your hike.

GETTING THERE

For the sake of brevity, driving directions begin from the nearest park entrance, or in some cases from the nearest town when there is no adjacent park entrance. This includes the park's West Entrance south of the intersection of Park Boulevard and State Route 62 in Joshua Tree, the park's North Entrance south of the intersection of the Utah Trail and SR 62 in Twentynine Palms, and the park's South Entrance north of Interstate 10. For Black Rock Canyon, Indian Cove, and Fortynine Palms, directions begin from the nearest town since there is no formal park entrance to refer to.

Note that access for a couple of routes in this guide requires driving on a dirt road. In normal conditions, all of these roads are safe for two-wheel-drive vehicles, although conditions can change following heavy rainfall. Contact the park in advance if you want to be absolutely sure that your two-wheel-drive vehicle can safely handle a specified dirt road.

Where applicable, the **Transit** section provides information based on the available RoadRunner Shuttle that services the busier sections of the park. Learn more at www .jtnproadrunner.org.

A NOTE ABOUT SAFETY

Safety is an important concern in all outdoor activities. No guidebook can alert you to every hazard or anticipate the limitations of every reader. Therefore, the descriptions of roads, trails, routes, and natural features in this book are not representations that a particular place or excursion will be safe for your party. When you follow any of the routes described in this book, you assume responsibility for your own safety. Under normal conditions, such excursions require the usual attention to traffic, road and trail conditions, weather, terrain, the capabilities of your party, and other factors. Keeping informed on current conditions and exercising common sense are the keys to a safe, enjoyable outing.

—*Mountaineers Books*

ON THE TRAIL

This section contains start-to-finish directions and highlights other notable features you'll need to know to complete and enjoy the hikes.

GOING FARTHER

This section offers additional directions that allow you to extend your route to nearby destinations. In some cases, this refers to alternate return routes or approaches.

Now that you're itching to get to Joshua Tree and start pounding some dirt, consider one last caution. Conditions in the desert change frequently. Although every effort has been made to ensure that this guide accurately reflects the conditions in the park, it is always wise to consult with rangers at the visitor centers before you set out. This best practice ensures that this guide works in tandem with the most recent on-the-ground information.

BLACK ROCK CANYON

Tucked away in the quiet northwest corner of the park, Black Rock Canyon presents an unexpected side of Joshua Tree National Park. Here on the western end of the Little San Bernardino Mountains, a habitat suspended somewhere between the desert and the mountains blankets the rugged, rolling landscape. While you'll see the same cacti, Joshua trees, and high-desert shrubs you'd expect throughout the rest of the Mojave, forests of pinyon pine, scrub oak, and mountain manzanita thrive here due to the region's slightly higher rainfall totals and higher elevations.

The combination of higher elevations and an intricate spiderweb of footpaths allows hikers to enjoy more opportunities in this region to find themselves high upon a windswept summit than anywhere else in the park. From these high points, vast, encompassing panoramas of Southern California's highest and lowest landmarks, ranging from the summit of Mount San Gorgonio to the depths of the Salton Sea, unfurl in an impressive spectacle of sand, sea, and sky.

Black Rock Campground and its nature center sit on the northern border of the park just south of the town of Yucca Valley. The campground is one of the few in Joshua Tree that accepts reservations, making it easier to plan trips in advance. Friendly rangers and volunteers in the nature center provide information, and a single backcountry registration board at the California Riding and Hiking Trailhead provides an access point for backpackers to penetrate the backcountry.

OPPOSITE *Mount San Jacinto rises from the wind farms of San Gorgonio Pass (Route 4).*

1   HIGH VIEW NATURE TRAIL

Distance: 1.3 miles (2.1 km)
Elevation gain: 350 feet (115 m)
High point: 4477 feet (1365 m)
Difficulty: Easy
Trail surface: Dirt
Map: USGS 7.5-minute Yucca Valley South
GPS: 34.076465° N, -116.399579° W
Notes: Day use only; good for kids; no restroom at trailhead; interpretive features

> Hikers eager to turn their children on to the wonders of desert peak bagging will find a nice introduction at the High View Nature Trail. This short interpretive loop provides excellent views of Black Rock Canyon and the San Bernardino Mountains by way of a quick climb to a breezy high point.

Mount San Gorgonio, a welcome scenic companion

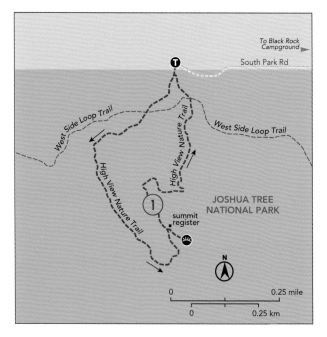

GETTING THERE

From the junction of Interstate 10 and State Route 62, head north toward Yucca Valley for 20.9 miles (33.6 km) to a junction with Joshua Lane. Turn right onto Joshua Lane and head south for 4.6 miles (7.4 km). Turn right onto San Marino Drive. San Marino Drive immediately turns left and becomes Black Rock Canyon Road. Just before the entrance to the main campground, turn right onto the unpaved South Park Road and follow it for 0.7 mile (1.1 km) to a parking area at the end of the road. The trailhead lies on the left side of the parking area.

ON THE TRAIL

From the signed trailhead, proceed south to a Y junction signaling the beginning of the looping High View Nature

Trail. Either path will get you to the top, but the right fork does so more gradually. After the right turn, immediately cross the West Side Loop Trail and continue on the trail as it arcs into a broad drainage. Views of Mount San Gorgonio to the west hint at the summit view, while interpretive panels at waist height illuminate hikers about the surrounding environs. Benches placed periodically along the trail offer opportunities to rest.

After climbing a rocky staircase, the trail turns north to follow a moderately steep slope to a prominent hilltop. This is the namesake "high view," where you'll find a summit register and a bench upon which to take a break. Be sure to leave a little wisdom in the register, and encourage any kids you have along with you to impart some inspired silliness. Fully realized views of Mount San Gorgonio inspire future peak-bagging opportunities as your youngsters grow older and become more accomplished hikers. A short spur trail leads southeast toward the highest point on the hill.

The return trip briefly follows the hill's northern ridgeline before bending right for a more gradual descent down the hillside. After one more crossing of the West Side Loop Trail at 1.2 miles (1.9 km), the trail ends where it began.

2 EUREKA PEAK

Distance: 9.6 miles (15.4 km)
Elevation gain: 1850 feet (565 m)
High point: 5518 feet (1682 m)
Difficulty: Challenging
Trail surface: Coarse sand and dirt
Maps: USGS 7.5-minute Yucca Valley South, Joshua Tree South
GPS: 34.075156° N, -116.387919° W
Notes: Suitable for backpacking; backcountry registration board; restrooms at Black Rock Nature Center

Joshua trees and soaring views are hallmarks of Eureka Peak.

This challenging all-day hike leads you to the highest point in the northwestern corner of the park. Although other peaks in the park are higher, none are as accessible nor do they provide quite as good a view of the Coachella Valley and Southern California's towering mountain ranges. This route also includes a short stretch of the historic California Riding and Hiking Trail, as well as the Little San Bernardino Mountains' abundant forests of pinyon pine, juniper, and Joshua trees.

GETTING THERE

From the junction of Interstate 10 and State Route 62, head north toward Yucca Valley for 20.9 miles (33.6 km) to a junction with Joshua Lane. Turn right onto Joshua Lane and head south for 4.6 miles (7.4 km). Turn right onto San Marino Drive. San Marino Drive immediately turns left and becomes Black Rock Canyon Road. Continue about 50 yards (46 m) past the campground entrance and find roadside parking, a trailhead kiosk, and a backcountry registration board for the California Riding and Hiking Trail.

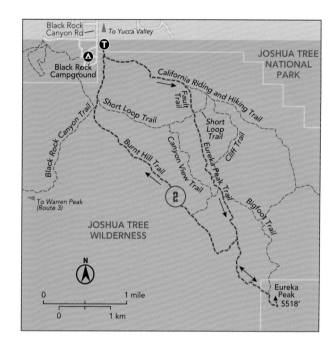

ON THE TRAIL

After locating the trailhead adjacent to the backcountry registration board, set foot on the opening stretch of Joshua Tree's portion of the historic California Riding and Hiking Trail (CRHT). Although the CRHT crosses the western two-thirds of the park, you'll remain on it only for a brief time before beginning the long ascent to Eureka Peak. After 0.2 mile (0.3 km), turn left onto the CRHT's sandy tread lined with wooden fences at the well-marked junction with the Black Rock Canyon Trail. From here, the trail begins a moderate ascent through a valley dotted with Joshua trees and pinyon pines and then crosses over a saddle to descend toward a junction with the Fault Trail at 1.3 miles (2.1 km).

Turn right onto the Fault Trail and begin a short, undulating traverse over jumbled terrain. At 1.7 miles (2.7 km), the Fault Trail bottoms out at a junction with the Short Loop Trail. Continue straight ahead on an unmarked but clear path for a 20-yard (18 m) walk to a wide wash that's marked as the Eureka Peak Trail. Join the wash and commence the moderate ascent to the peak through a sheltered canyon graced by impressively large pinyon pines and scrub oaks.

With loose sand occasionally retarding your pace, continue uphill, nearly due south through this remarkably straight drainage. As you progress, you will pass through junctions with the Cliff Trail on the left (2.6 miles, 4.2 km), the Canyon View Trail on the right (2.75 miles, 4.4 km), an unmarked spur of the Bigfoot Trail on the left (2.85 miles, 4.6 km), and finally the Burnt Hill Trail on the right (3.5 miles, 5.6 km).

The arid expanse of Yucca Valley viewed from Warren Peak

THE CALIFORNIA RIDING
AND HIKING TRAIL

Long before the genesis of America's great national scenic trails, such as the Pacific Crest Trail and Appalachian Trail, California's government conceived the idea of a looping network of trails running up the coast and back down the Golden State's mountainous spine. An unending series of private property conflicts ultimately doomed the project, but trail builders were able to complete significant sections of the trail in the Southern California deserts. Joshua Tree National Park contains one of the longest uninterrupted stretches of the CRHT in the state, and backpackers can follow the trail from its beginning at Black Rock Canyon to its terminus at the park's North Entrance south of Twentynine Palms.

Beyond the Burnt Hill Trail, the wash narrows and steepens until you find yourself huffing and puffing to the top of a saddle at 4.4 miles (7.1 km). A side trail leads away on the left to what looks like a peak, but don't be fooled. There's still one more saddle to cross before the final ascent. Dip down past another junction with the Bigfoot Trail and cross over that final saddle between peak 5418 and Eureka Peak. Views up to this point have been scant due to the passage through canyons and woodlands, and the sudden reveal of the foothills of the Little San Bernardinos melting into the Coachella Valley is both an arresting and inspiring sight. The towering ramparts of the San Jacinto and Santa Rosa Mountains, which may be frosted with snow during the winter, loom high over the desert cities.

At 4.7 miles (7.6 km), the Eureka Peak Trail terminates at a T junction. A left turn leads you to the summit, from which point you can enjoy the panoramic views encompassing the park, the San Jacintos, and Southern California's high point, Mount San Gorgonio to the west. A right turn at the T junction leads to the end of Eureka Peak Road, which hikers in four-wheel-drive vehicles can follow to access the peak.

For the return trip, head back to the junction with the Burnt Hill Trail and hook a left. Follow the trail up and out of a shallow valley and then down into a major tributary canyon feeding Black Rock Canyon that features a dense forest of Joshua trees. The Burnt Hill Trail merges into the Black Rock Canyon Trail at 8.8 miles (14.2 km), which you can follow all the way back to the first junction with the CRHT. Keep left there to return to your car.

3   WARREN PEAK

Distance: 5.2 miles (8.4 km)
Elevation gain: 1090 feet (335 m)
High point: 5103 feet (1555 m)
Difficulty: Moderate
Trail surface: Dirt and coarse sand
Map: USGS 7.5-minute Yucca Valley South
GPS: 34.071569° N, -116.390896° W
Notes: Day use only; restroom adjacent to trailhead within campground or at Black Rock Nature Center

Although Southern California's highest points, Mount San Jacinto and Mount San Gorgonio, make cameo appearances on many hikes throughout Joshua Tree, the windswept heights of Warren Peak offer the best vistas of the twin behemoths. The soaring views contrast with a pleasant hike through Black Rock Canyon's forest of Joshua trees, pinyon pines, scrub oak, and juniper that culminates in the final short, sharp summit ascent.

GETTING THERE

From the junction of Interstate 10 and State Route 62, head north toward Yucca Valley for 20.9 miles (33.6 km) to a junction with Joshua Lane. Turn right onto Joshua Lane and head south for 4.6 miles (7.4 km). Turn right onto San Marino Drive. San Marino Drive immediately turns left and becomes Black Rock Canyon Road. Continue straight onto Campground Road, and continue to campsite 30 on the south end of the campground. Park at one of a handful of day-use parking spots and find the trailhead adjacent to the campsite.

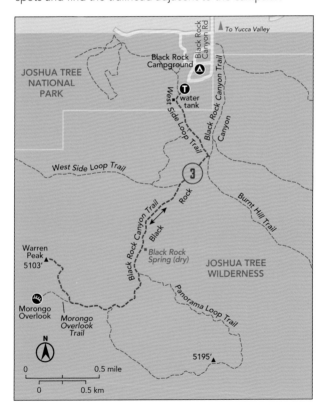

Black Rock Canyon melts away to the vast expanse of the Mojave Desert.

ON THE TRAIL

From the trailhead next to campsite 30, head due south on an eroded dirt road, and keep left at a junction with the West Side Loop Trail. Shortly thereafter, keep left again at the access road to the water tank to begin descending into Black Rock Canyon. At the 0.6-mile (1 km) mark, you merge with the Black Rock Canyon Trail. Keep right to avoid inadvertently taking the Burnt Hill Trail to the left.

As you progress up Black Rock Canyon's wide wash, keep your eyes peeled for a couple of highlights along the way. At 1.2 miles (1.9 km), twin outcrops of black gneiss striated with layers of white herald the narrowing of Black Rock Canyon while dropping hints about where the canyon got its name. You will reach Black Rock Spring at 1.4 miles (2.3 km). Although the topo maps indicate that the spring is dry, you may find just enough water to provide a big gulp for a thirsty mountain lion.

Beyond the spring, the canyon narrows as the path continues along the wash. At a well-defined and signed Y junction with the Panorama Trail at 1.6 miles, keep right and proceed to the second branch of the Panorama Loop Trail at 1.9 miles

(3.1 km). Turn right at this second junction, and continue climbing on a gradually steeper pitch to a final junction with the Morongo Overlook Trail nestled within a lovely, broad valley. Keep right one final time at this junction to commence the steep ascent to Warren Peak at 2.6 miles (4.2 km).

The summit vista reveals a full panorama of sights you caught only glimpses of along the approach. Mount San Jacinto and the serrated Desert Divide tower above the desert communities of the Coachella Valley while the often snow-dusted summit of Mount San Gorgonio looms due west. The startling western view reveals a precipitous descent into the convoluted canyons and ridges of the Little San Bernardino Mountains below. An equally complex system of peaks and valleys leads away east toward Eureka and Quail Peaks.

GOING FARTHER

The Morongo Overlook Trail leads you on a gentler approach to a lower point that could serve as a consolation prize for folks who shy away from the last steep pitch to the summit. Also, you can add on the Panorama Loop for a longer return trip. This detour adds an additional 2.1 miles (3.4 km) and 600 feet of elevation gain to the route.

4 PANORAMA LOOP

Distance: 5.9 miles (9.5 km)
Elevation gain: 1200 feet (365 m)
High point: 5195 feet (1583 m)
Difficulty: Moderate
Trail surface: Coarse sand and dirt
Map: USGS 7.5-minute Yucca Valley South
GPS: 34.071569° N, -116.390896° W
Notes: Day use only; restroom adjacent to trailhead within campground or at Black Rock Nature Center

One of the beautiful old Joshua trees on the Panorama Loop

This moderate half-day hike delivers exactly what the name implies: panoramic views. The sweeping vistas in every direction are every bit as good as anything you will find in Joshua Tree. The mix of highlights along the way includes intriguing outcrops of ancient metamorphic rock, serene passages through Black Rock Canyon's forests of pinyons, junipers, and Joshua trees, and a descent through a beautiful, grassy valley blessed with sweeping views of the surrounding mountains.

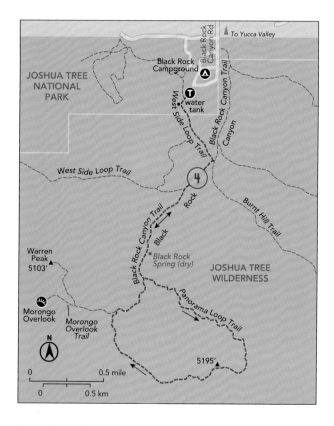

GETTING THERE

From the junction of Interstate 10 and State Route 62, head north toward Yucca Valley for 20.9 miles (33.6 km) to a junction with Joshua Lane. Turn right onto Joshua Lane and head south for 4.6 miles (7.4 km). Turn right onto San Marino Drive. San Marino Drive immediately turns left and becomes Black Rock Canyon Road. Continue straight onto Campground Road, and continue to campsite 30 on the south end of the campground. Park at one of a handful of

PANORAMA LOOP ✦ 81

day-use parking spots and find the trailhead adjacent to the campsite.

ON THE TRAIL

From the trailhead next to campsite 30, head due south on an eroded dirt road, and keep left at a junction with the West Side Loop Trail. Shortly thereafter, keep left again at the access road to the water tank to begin descending into Black Rock Canyon. At the 0.6-mile (1 km) mark, you merge with the Black Rock Canyon Trail. Keep right to avoid inadvertently taking the Burnt Hill Trail to the left.

As you progress up Black Rock Canyon's wide wash, keep your eyes peeled for a couple of highlights along the way. At 1.2 miles (1.9 km), twin outcrops of black gneiss striated with layers of white herald the narrowing of Black Rock Canyon while dropping hints about where the canyon got its name. You will reach Black Rock Spring at 1.4 miles (2.3 km). Although the topo maps indicate that the spring is dry, you may find just enough water to provide a big gulp for a thirsty mountain lion.

After the spring, the canyon narrows significantly before making a pronounced split at 1.6 miles. The left branch is the beginning of the Panorama Loop, while the right branch will be your return route. Turn left and begin climbing up-canyon through a brief narrow and rocky stretch. Beautiful outcrops of gneiss line the canyon walls on both sides. Note the various spots where plants such as hedgehog cactus, scrub oak, pinyon, and juniper have established a toehold within cracks in the rocks. Their root systems find pockets of soil filling nooks and crannies that hang on to water long enough to sustain plant life.

After this short, narrow stretch, the canyon widens into a small hidden valley graced with abundant Joshua trees and junipers. At 2.4 miles (3.9 km), the grade of the trail steepens considerably as it climbs a ridge toward peak 5195. Occasional stops to catch your breath grant opportunities to soak in the view north across Yucca Valley. The ascent eases at 2.7 miles (4.3 km), at which point you enjoy a short stretch of ridgeline walking as you approach the base of peak 5195. From this high point, you can enjoy the Panorama Loop in the truest sense of its name. Mount San Jacinto and Mount San Gorgonio dominate the southern and western vista, with the wooded peaks and valleys surrounding you melting southward into the Coachella Valley.

After enjoying the peak, begin your return journey on a lovely and tranquil descent to the west through a broad, grassy valley dotted with Joshua trees and pinyons. Views toward Mount San Gorgonio transition to views toward nearby Warren Peak as the trail descends. At 3.9 miles (6.3 km), you arrive at a junction with the trail to Warren Peak, at which point you'll continue straight ahead unless you want to take an optional trip to the peak. Turn right here and continue descending to the first branch of the Panorama Loop

HEY, GNEISS ROCKS!

A short jaunt up Black Rock Canyon quickly reveals a hint as to how the canyon got its name. Outcrops of metamorphic sedimentary rock known as gneiss line the washes and canyon walls of the mountains in the region. The canyon's gneiss displays striking layers of black rock alternating with striations of lighter-colored rocks. Although monzogranite is the "rock star" of Joshua Tree's geology (pun absolutely intended), these ancient outcrops of gneiss, dating back to over a billion years ago, look on with detached amusement at the much younger igneous upstarts of Queen Valley and Lost Horse Valley. Never forget the eternal eye-roller: "If you meet a gneiss rock, don't take it for granite!"

and then past Black Rock Spring all the way back to the campground.

GOING FARTHER

If time and energy permit, you can tack on a trip to Warren Peak (Route 3). Factor in an additional 1.4 miles (2.3 km) and another 500 feet (150 m) of climbing for this diversion.

WEST ENTRANCE

Even though Joshua Tree's West Entrance receives so much vehicle traffic that the park recently commenced a shuttle service to mitigate congestion, the majority of the trails between the entrance and Keys Ranch remain surprisingly quiet. From various trailheads along Park Boulevard between the park entrance and Hidden Valley, hikers can enjoy a diverse array of hiking experiences ranging from cross-country explorations, rambling traverses through rugged and complex landscapes, and historical oddities that recall Joshua Tree's colorful past.

Only two signed trailheads offer restrooms or picnic areas within this section of the park: the Quail Springs picnic area and the Boy Scout Trail staging area. Of those two, the Boy Scout Trail is the only trailhead in this section with a backcountry registration board. The remainder of the trailheads offer limited parking and lack clear signage announcing their presence, which may contribute to the relative lack of traffic on the area's trails.

Visitors looking for information can visit the Joshua Tree Visitor Center north of the park entrance in the town of Joshua Tree. Here you can get information and advice from helpful rangers and volunteers, and you can also pick up additional literature on the park while perusing the center's exhibits.

OPPOSITE *The eminently appealing Maze Trail (Route 6) at its most mazelike*

5   NORTH VIEW TRAIL

Distance: 5.1 miles (8.2 km)
Elevation gain: 1070 feet (325 m)
High point: 4437 feet (1352 m)
Difficulty: Moderate
Trail surface: Coarse sand
Map: USGS 7.5-minute Indian Cove
GPS: 34.081096° N, -116.242396° W
Notes: Day use only; limited parking; no restroom at trailhead

> This rugged loop encircles the jagged, fractured high country bounding the northern edge of the park. You will find plenty of fine examples of the promised views north toward Joshua Tree and beyond to the expansive flats of the Mojave. Closer at hand, you will enjoy abundant examples of the park's famous geology at every step.

GETTING THERE

From the park's West Entrance, south of the town of Joshua Tree, head south on Park Boulevard for 1.8 miles (2.9 km) to the Maze Loop Trailhead on the left side of the road.

ON THE TRAIL

The start for this hike is a bit confusing, but if you pay close attention to the signage, you should be able to find your way with minimal difficulty. Walk straight from the parking area and ignore the trail junctions for the North Side Trail and south access for the Maze Loop Trail that pop up after 30 yards (27 m). After skirting an old gravel pit for another 100 yards (90 m), keep right at a second junction for the North Side Trail before reaching the North View Trail another 200 yards (180 m) later. Turn left here to leave the rapid-fire junctions behind.

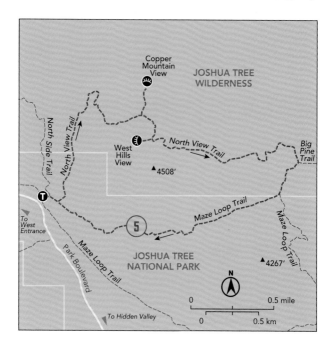

Over the next 2.9 miles (4.7 km), the North View Trail twists, turns, climbs, and then undulates through some exceptionally rugged country. At 0.9 mile (1.4 km), the trail bottoms out in a secluded, hidden drainage dominated by varnished granite outcroppings eroded into fabulous shapes. This section offers some good views north, especially as you commence a prolonged climb over the next 0.5 mile (0.8 km) to a junction with a 0.5-mile (0.8 km) roundtrip spur trail leading to Copper Mountain View. This vista point at the end of the spur features the best northern views on the route.

After the spur, trudge through the last big climb on the route to reach the West Hills View spur trail at 2 miles (3.2 km) from the start. This 0.3-mile (0.5 km) roundtrip spur trail

Monzogranite formations upstage the views north on the North View Trail.

leads to a spot overlooking the rugged terrain bounding Quail Springs Wash to the west. From here, the trail crests the route's high point before descending along a somewhat convoluted path into and then out of a wash at 2.9 miles (4.7 km).

Continue past a junction with the Big Pine Trail on the left at 3.2 miles (5.1 km). From here, the trail meanders through rolling country studded with Joshua trees, Mojave yucca, and a host of different shrubs and cacti before arriving at a Y junction with the Maze Loop at 3.4 miles (5.5 km).

Turn right onto the northern branch of the Maze Loop, which returns you to the start of the North View Trail at 5 miles (8 km). From there, retrace your steps past the North Side Trail junctions to return to your vehicle.

GOING FARTHER

You can combine the North View Trail with the Maze and Windows Loop Trails (see Route 6) for a 7.2-mile (11.6 km) route gaining 975 feet (295 m) of elevation.

6   MAZE-WINDOWS LOOP

Distance: 5.9 miles (9.5 km)
Elevation gain: 680 feet (210 m)
High point: 4270 feet (1300 m)
Difficulty: Moderate
Trail surface: Coarse sand and occasional rock
Map: USGS 7.5-minute Indian Cove
GPS: 34.081096° N, -116.242396° W
Notes: Day use only; limited parking; no restroom at trailhead

> Despite the intimidating name, this route is one of the more accessible in the West Entrance region. A winning combination of Joshua tree woodland, appealing rock formations, a relatively mild amount of uphill work, and great views across Lost Horse Valley make this meandering route a great place to begin your explorations of the West Entrance trail network. Just be sure to stick to the trail unless you really want to find out why they call it "the Maze."

GETTING THERE

From the park's West Entrance, south of the town of Joshua Tree, head south on Park Boulevard for 1.8 miles (2.9 km) to the Maze Loop Trailhead on the left side of the road.

ON THE TRAIL

Although this route has garnered a reputation for being a dangerous place due to several lost hikers requiring rescues, including one tragic situation where two hikers died after becoming lost during a mid-July hike, the actual routefinding is not as difficult as the name implies. Well-marked trails lace the area, with only a few spots needing routefinding consideration. The trouble seems to occur when people leave the main trail to scramble on rocks or explore side trips. Keep to the trail and pay close attention to the trail signs and markers, and you should have no trouble.

Head east on the brief connector trail departing Park Boulevard. You quickly encounter a trio of trail junctions in rapid succession. At the first junction, with the south access trail for the Maze Loop and the North Side Trail, stay straight. At

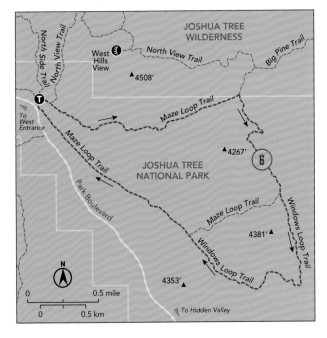

The Windows Loop Trail offers a classic glimpse into Lost Horse Valley.

the next two junctions, the second leg of the North Side Trail and the North View Trail, keep right. After those junctions, you continue east along a wide sandy wash that climbs at a gentle rate to a saddle at 1.3 miles (2.1 km) between peak 4508 to the north and peak 4627 to the south. Continue east from the saddle for a short 0.4-mile (0.6 km) descent to a junction with the eastern branch of the North View Trail at 1.7 miles (2.7 km).

Turn right to continue on the Maze Loop. Just beyond the junction, you will encounter the most mazelike section of the route as the trail weaves and wends through a picturesque boulder garden punctuated by junipers and Joshua trees. As you progress, your first glimpses east toward Lost Horse Valley and the rolling heights of Ryan Mountain appear. These views stay with you until the Windows Loop Trail turns west later on, and they improve as you go.

Hikers looking for a shorter loop can turn right onto the southern branch of the Maze Loop Trail at 2.7 miles (4.3 km). This shortcut follows a wash west toward Park Boulevard before turning northwest on the return branch of the Maze Loop toward the parking lot. This shorter route shaves a mile and about 200 feet (60 m) of elevation gain off the hike. If you're taking the full Maze-Windows Loop, the Windows portion wraps around to the south of peak 4381 before turning northwest toward the parking area. You get the finest views east on the route at 2.9 miles (4.7 km) before the trail weaves through a series of drainages on its way back to the beginning.

The final leg of the loop heads due northwest on a nearly flat grade through a valley dotted with prominent boulder piles. At 5.9 miles (9.5 km), turn left to follow the short connector back to the parking area.

GOING FARTHER
You can combine this route with the North View Trail (Route 5) for a 7.2-mile (11.6 km) roundtrip hike gaining 975 feet (295 m) of elevation.

7   BIGFOOT-PANORAMA LOOP

Distance: 7 miles (11.3 km)
Elevation gain: 1400 feet (425 m)
High point: 4269 feet (1301 m)
Difficulty: Challenging
Trail surface: Dirt with occasional rock outcrops followed by extended sections of sandy wash
Maps: USGS 7.5-minute Indian Cove, Joshua Tree South
GPS: 34.077847° N, -116.240911° W
Notes: Day use only; navigation required; moderately difficult terrain; limited parking; no restroom at trailhead

Most routes that get you off the beaten path in Joshua Tree require extensive cross-country travel and a lot of navigational expertise. However, the Bigfoot-Panorama Loop offers

> a middle ground: a slightly beaten path with less-severe navigational challenges. Aside from the obvious reward of solitude despite being a few direct miles from the busiest thoroughfare in the park, you will also enjoy some stunning views surveying the park's rugged and lonely interior.

GETTING THERE

From the park's West Entrance, south of the town of Joshua Tree, head south on Park Boulevard for 2 miles (3.2 km) to an unsigned trailhead with an unnamed connector trail leading to the Bigfoot Trail on the left side of the road.

ON THE TRAIL

Follow the sandy connector trail west-southwest up and over a saddle before dropping into a broad wash at 0.4 mile

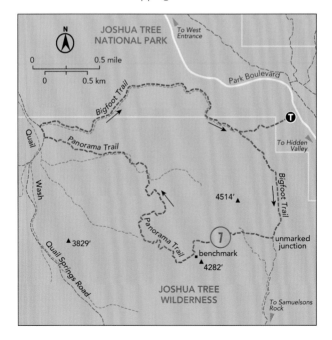

Cloudy with a slight chance of Sasquatches on the Bigfoot Trail

(0.6 km). At this point, you get to pick your poison regarding which challenge you'd like to face. A left turn for a clockwise loop follows a well-defined but unmarked trail south that ends with a prolonged trudge uphill through a sandy wash. A right turn for a counterclockwise loop allows an easier descent through the sandy wash only to face a prolonged climb with a few confusing twists and turns thrown in for seasoning. If you're okay with this author choosing your poison for you, turn left and begin a moderate ascent along the Bigfoot Trail.

After cresting a saddle at 0.9 mile (1.4 km), you begin enjoying stellar views south toward Quail Mountain and Johnny Lang Canyon as well as east toward Lost Horse Valley. Be sure not to get too lost in the views and the easy downhill stroll that follows, or else you may miss the unmarked junction with the Panorama Trail at 1.4 miles (2.3 km). If you find yourself suddenly on the valley floor with the hills behind you, you've gone too far and need to turn around.

Turn right onto the Panorama Trail and begin a moderate climb punctuated by occasional dips into and out of washes. The tread can be a little vague at times on this section, requiring consistent attention. Keep an eye out for the USGS benchmark just northwest from peak 4282 at 2.1 miles (3.4 km). The magnificent view toward Quail Mountain and down into Quail Wash provides an obvious hint as to why the USGS chose this spot for surveying. Although there are more views to enjoy should you continue, the benchmark is a good turnaround spot for hikers who want an easier hike without sacrificing all of the route's highlights. If that sounds like you, turn around at the benchmark and retrace your steps to the trailhead.

After a bit more climbing beyond the 4282 benchmark, the trail begins a prolonged descent into Quail Wash. The first mile of this descent continues along a well-defined trail, which gives you a chance to enjoy the views north over Yucca Valley and west toward Mount San Gorgonio. At 3.5 miles (5.6 km), the trail joins a wash only to pop out again about 100 yards (90 m) later. After a brief detour around a rocky section of the wash, the trail disintegrates into the wash for good, and for nearly the reminder of the route, you'll be following washes on soft sand. Continue downhill and avoid thinking too much about the uphill climb ahead that begins where the trail bottoms out at Quail Wash at 4.5 miles (7.2 km).

After turning right onto Quail Wash, walk north for about 100 yards (90 m) into a tributary wash leading east. This wash represents another portion of the unmaintained Bigfoot Trail, and you will follow it all the way back to a connector trail that leads back to Park Boulevard. The steady and sandy prolonged climb encounters no junctions until 5.9 miles (9.5 km), at which point you bear right where the wash splits. The wash splits again at 6.3 miles (10.1 km), and this time you'll bear left. Finally, at 6.6 miles (10.6 km), you will find yourself at the junction with the connector trail back to the parking area. Turn left here to climb up and over the saddle and back down to your car.

GOING FARTHER

If you have the time and energy, you can continue heading south on the Bigfoot Trail past the Panorama Trail junction, toward Samuelsons Rock. Here, you will find some grammatically suspect philosophy etched into the desert varnish by John Samuelson, one of the many desert eccentrics who occupied Joshua Tree before it became a park. This detour adds 2.6 miles (4.2 km) roundtrip and 300 feet (90 m) of elevation gain to the overall route.

8 QUAIL MOUNTAIN

Distance: 10.2 miles (16.4 km)
Elevation gain: 2600 feet (790 m)
High point: 5813 feet (1772 m)
Difficulty: Strenuous
Trail surface: Dirt and rock
Map: USGS 7.5-minute Indian Cove
GPS: 34.056112° N, -116.220824° W
Notes: Day use only; navigation required; difficult terrain; no restroom at trailhead; historical interest

What serious peak bagger can resist the siren call of a superlative high point? Even though you can obtain similar views at nearby summits for a fraction of the effort, there's nothing quite like conquering the highest spot in the park while standing head and shoulders above the rest. If you're not one to let a calorie-annihilating cross-country approach get between you and a lofty peak, follow this strenuous route to the summit of Quail Mountain.

GETTING THERE

From the park's West Entrance, drive southeast on Park Boulevard for 3.9 miles (6.3 km) to a pull-out parking area on the north (left) side of the road. If you're coming directly from the West Entrance, you will need to make a U-turn, which is safest if you drive beyond to the Quail Springs picnic area and turn around from there.

ON THE TRAIL

To begin, cross Park Boulevard to reach the south side of the road. There is no formal trailhead, but look for a faint informal path. The path doesn't last long, and for the first mile of

A Mojave mound cactus blossom posing for the camera

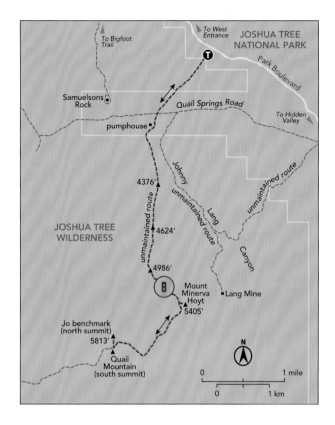

this route, you navigate through open Joshua tree woodland across a gently sloping valley. Set your sites on a prominent ridge bounding the western side of Johnny Lang Canyon by heading due southwest from the parking area. You will see a small hill that's darker than the surrounding slopes at the mouth of Johnny Lang Canyon. If you don't see it at first, it will become more apparent the closer you get to the canyon. Aim for the right (west) edge of that hill so that you can continue to the foot of a long, prominent ridge that runs due south toward the rounded summit of Quail Mountain.

After crossing the old Quail Springs roadbed at 1 mile (1.6 km), continue past that hill, and keep an eye out for an informal path that leads to a well just south of Johnny Lang Canyon's wash. An old water pump stands under the shelter of an open shack, and piping pours the water (which still flows!) into an old trough. The water in the trough looks deeply unappealing, so be sure to bring plenty of your own. Continue southwest to the foot of the ridge at 1.2 miles (1.9 km), and start climbing.

The climb begins along an undulating ridge punctuated with a number of rocky outcrops. Although there are disjointed traces of cairn-marked, informal footpaths following the spine of the ridge, the cairns are spaced so irregularly that it's very difficult to keep to it. Your best strategy on tackling the small-scale routefinding that the unreliable cairns create is to follow the spine of the ridge, keep to the cairns where possible, and circumvent the outcrops by traversing the slopes just below them. You may have more luck keeping to the west side of the ridge's spine, owing to the gentler slopes on that side.

The exception to the "keep slightly west of the ridgeline" strategy arrives at 3 miles (4.8 km) when you reach the base of peak 4986. Either go straight over this peak or keep slightly to the east to reach a saddle southeast of the peak. Once at this saddle, you will find yourself face-to-face with Quail Mountain's suddenly formidable summit block. However, thanks to a deep canyon and extreme slope between you and the summit, you're better off taking a mildly heartbreaking detour around the head of the canyon by way of Mount Minerva Hoyt (peak 5405) due southeast from peak 4986. Climb the steep slope, keeping to the west of the ridgeline along a track marked by haphazard cairns. At 3.7 miles (6 km), you reach the shoulder of Mount Minerva Hoyt, which you can tackle if you've got some energy and time to burn.

Beyond Mount Minerva Hoyt, you will drop to another saddle, due south, at which point you will find a much more reliable path beaten down by boot traffic. This footpath begins a gradual 0.6-mile (1 km) descent that you'll have some choice words for on the return journey. The descent bottoms out at the top of a shallow ravine before resuming the climb on a slope leading southwest toward Quail Mountain's eastern summit ridge.

You reach the eastern ridge at 4.7 miles (7.6 km). Turn right here to follow the informal trail west toward the summit. At 5 miles (8 km), the trail bends to the south and leads to the highest point on the summit block. The south peak has the best views south toward Mount San Jacinto and east across Juniper Flat and Lost Horse Valley. For an extension of the view, head north about 50 yards (46 m) to another rock pile marking the northern summit. Here, you'll find "Jo" benchmark, as well as great views north toward Queen Mountain and the Wonderland of Rocks.

On the return journey, watch out for the junction where the path turns back northward toward Mount Minerva Hoyt. It's easy to fall into a groove heading downhill, which may cause you to miss the junction and could lead you down the wrong ridge toward Juniper Flat, as well as cause a lot of extra walking and much exercising of colorful vocabulary.

9 JOHNNY LANG CANYON

Distance: 6 miles (9.7 km)
Elevation gain: 630 feet (190 m)
High point: 4342 feet (1324 m)
Difficulty: Challenging
Trail surface: Sandy, unmaintained, followed by progressively rockier wash and occasional stretches of open desert
Map: USGS 7.5-minute Indian Cove

GPS: 34.040427° N, -116.198280° W

Notes: Day use only; navigation required; moderately difficult terrain; pit toilets at trailhead; historical interest

> Silence, solitude, and a serving of park history are on the menu with this rambling walkabout through the confines of Johnny Lang Canyon. Dust off your map and compass skills to follow a historic roadbed into the canyon to reach Lang's homestead site and nearby mine before returning via a network of washes—a satisfying ramble through a quiet corner of the park.

GETTING THERE

From the park's West Entrance, drive southeast on Park Boulevard for 5.8 miles (9.3 km) to the Quail Springs picnic area

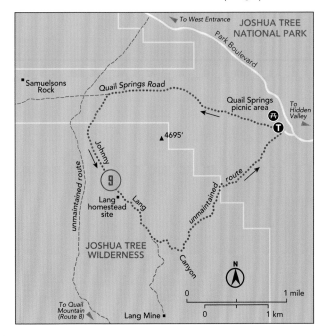

A metamorphic pileup in Johnny Lang Canyon

on the west side of the road. Turn right on the access road to the picnic area, and continue toward the parking area. The unmarked trailhead lies just south of the restrooms.

ON THE TRAIL

After finding the unheralded beginning of historic Quail Springs Road, head west on the gently descending track as it approaches and then skirts the base of peak 4695. The trail can be hard to follow, especially where it crosses washes. If you find yourself wandering too far north along a parallel wash, cut south toward the hills, and eventually you will reach the trail again. You may notice a number of blackened Joshua trees in an expansive burn zone, and some of these dead trees may cross the path to present minor obstacles.

At 2 miles (3.2 km), turn left onto an unmarked junction to follow the remains of an old jeep road into Johnny Lang Canyon. At around the 3-mile (4.8 km) mark, keep your eyes peeled for the rusted remains of Lang's homestead. See if you can spot the lone cottonwood in the wash. These thirsty trees require abundant water, which suggests that there is water close to the surface that perhaps the homestead used. The trail becomes less well defined and a bit harder to follow until you leave it entirely at 3.7 miles (6 km) in favor of the wash. Although the trail does continue toward Lang Mine, you will veer left here to follow the wash as it meanders in a generally southeast direction. If you're uncomfortable with cross-country navigation, this is a good spot to turn back and retrace your steps to the trailhead.

The vegetation in the wash and on the surrounding hillsides undergoes a dramatic transformation at the 4-mile (6.4 km) mark. After bearing left here where the wash splits, the previously rolling hills transition into heavily fractured granite ringing an amphitheater-like valley. Thickets of scrub oak and pinyon pine remind you that you're in the high desert, while occasionally causing you to leave the wash to circumvent their scratchy branches. At 4.1 miles (6.6 km), you leave this intriguing valley behind on a short but steep scramble to a saddle due north at 4.4 miles (7.1 km).

From the saddle, work your way north across a rugged drainage to the bottom of a broad draw that becomes a narrow and rocky wash at 5 miles (8 km). You will continue downhill along this wash with occasional scrambling over jumbled rocks until the wash opens up into a broad plain. Head due northeast over a sandy ridge that may be speckled with sand verbena following wet winters. Once atop this ridge, continue northeast, perhaps finding an informal trail at 5.75 miles (9.3 km) that will take you back to the Quail Springs picnic area.

10 BOY SCOUT TRAIL

Distance: 8 miles (12.9 km)
Elevation gain: 375 feet (115 m)
High point: 4185 feet (1275 m)
Difficulty: Challenging
Trail surface: Mostly hard-packed sand with a long stretch of soft sand within a wash
Map: USGS 7.5-minute Indian Cove
GPS: 34.041397° N, -116.186081° W
Notes: Suitable for backpacking; pit toilet at trailhead; back-country registration board at trailhead

Set aside a cool winter's day for this spectacular mostly downhill route running from the Keys West Trailhead to the Boy Scout Trailhead in Indian Cove. Although the logistics require that you leave a car at both trailheads, the one-way route allows you to enjoy a dramatic transition from high Joshua-tree-dotted valleys ringed with rock piles into a rugged canyon that deposits you within Indian Cove, just north of its namesake campground.

GETTING THERE

Driving to Keys West Trailhead: From the town of Joshua Tree, head east on State Route 62, and turn right onto Park Boulevard. Continue south for 5.2 miles (8.4 km) to the park's West Entrance. From the entrance, drive another 6.5 miles (10.5 km) east until you reach the signed trailhead for the Boy Scout Trail on the north (left) side of the road.

Morning light paints the ramparts of Indian Cove.

Driving to Boy Scout Trailhead (end point): From the town of Joshua Tree, head east for 9.1 miles (14.6 km). Turn right onto Indian Cove Road, and head south for 1.7 miles (2.7 km) to the Boy Scout Trailhead.

Transit: The RoadRunner Shuttle (Joshua Tree–Jumbo Rocks) stops at the Keys West Trailhead every two hours.

ON THE TRAIL

The popular Boy Scout Trail serves as a backpacking route, but please note that everything east of the trail—including the Wonderland of Rocks and Willow Hole—is open for day use only. Backpackers must pitch their tents west of the trail. If you plan to enjoy this route as an overnight trip, be sure to register first and leave a copy of your registration visible in your car.

After settling the car shuttle challenge for this one-way hike, head north from the Keys West Trailhead along the Boy Scout Trail's nearly flat, sandy tread. The opening stretch of this hike passes sporadic boulder piles and through Joshua tree forests as it skirts the western margins of the Wonderland of Rocks. As you keep left at the junction with the Willow Hole Trail at 1.3 miles (2.1 km), you may look on longingly as the stunning Wonderland of Rocks shimmers in the distance. Long not, as many fantastic formations lie ahead.

After about 3.2 miles (5.1 km) of easy walking through the Joshua trees, the trail reaches the southern edge of Keys Peak, at which point the landscape gradually transitions from open valley to rugged drainages. The trail begins descending upon entering a gradually narrowing wash lined with pinyon pines

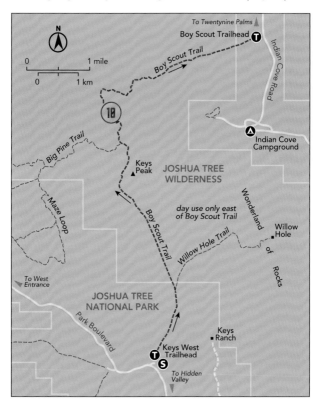

Northbound on the Boy Scout Trail

and Muller oaks before arriving at a junction with the Big Pine Trail at 4 miles (6.4 km). Shortly beyond this junction, the trail begins undulating in and out of a handful of ravines that lace a magnificently bewildering garden of towering rock piles. At 4.6 miles (7.4 km), the trail crests a saddle and begins a steep descent into a sinuous canyon.

This switchbacking descent will rattle your knees until it bottoms out in a wash at 5 miles (8 km). Although the hard downhill work is over, you now face a long stretch of walking through soft sand. The rocky canyon walls and general loveliness of this mid-elevation desert wilderness is enough compensation for the hard work, and after several twists and turns through heavily fractured granite corridors, the trail leaves the wash for good at 6.3 miles (10.1 km).

The remaining 1.7 miles (2.7 km) to the Boy Scout Trailhead traverse open middle-elevation desert dominated by creosote, pencil cholla, jojoba, and abundant wildflowers during March and early April. The northern ramparts of the Wonderland of Rocks melt into Indian Cove's sheltered basin to the south, providing one last burst of granitic splendor before you reach your car.

GOING FARTHER

Hikers can take a side trip to Willow Hole for a 4.8-mile (7.7 km) diversion. See Route 11 for details.

11   WILLOW HOLE

Distance: 7 miles (11.3 km)
Elevation gain: 300 feet (90 m)
High point: 4163 feet (1269 m)
Difficulty: Moderate
Trail surface: Hard-packed sand on the Boy Scout Trail; soft sand in the wash
Map: USGS 7.5-minute Indian Cove
GPS: 34.041397° N, -116.186081° W
Notes: Minor routefinding to navigate wash to Willow Hole; pit toilet at trailhead; backcountry registration board at trailhead

Stunning and bewildering in equal measure, the Wonderland of Rocks provides Joshua Tree's finest examples of towering monzogranite rock piles. Numerous washes weave through this sprawling wilderness of stone, creating the sort of navigational challenges that frighten off even the most experienced hikers. Fortunately, a relatively straightforward route by way of the Willow Hole Trail penetrates the Wonderland, leading you to a surprising oasis of willows bounded by fantastic granite formations.

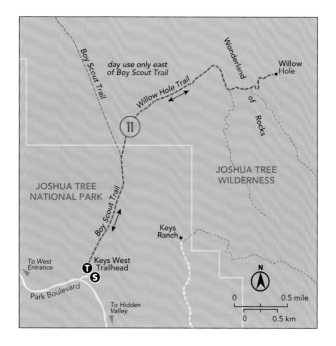

GETTING THERE

Driving: From the town of Joshua Tree, head east on State Route 62, and turn right onto Park Boulevard. Continue south for 5.2 miles (8.4 km) to the park's West Entrance. From the entrance, drive another 6.5 miles (10.5 km) east until you reach the signed trailhead for the Boy Scout Trail on the north (left) side of the road.

   Transit: The RoadRunner Shuttle (Joshua Tree–Jumbo Rocks) stops at the Keys West Trailhead every two hours.

ON THE TRAIL

From its southern terminus, the Boy Scout Trail travels north along the western edge of the Wonderland of Rocks before following a canyon into Indian Cove. This popular trail also

Monzogranite on the Willow Hole Trail

serves as a backpacking route, but please note that everything east of the trail—including the Wonderland of Rocks
and Willow Hole—is open for day use only. Backpackers
must pitch their tents west of the trail. If you plan to enjoy
this route as an overnight trip, be sure to register first and
leave a copy of your registration visible in your car.

Strike out north along the Boy Scout Trail for a pleasant,
nearly flat amble through Joshua tree woodland. As you
progress, the ramparts on the western edge of the Wonderland of Rocks draw closer. The rugged, jumbled hillsides
and boulder piles provide countless tutorials on the artistry
of the combined erosional forces of time and water. At
1.3 miles (2.1 km), you reach both the edge of the Wonderland and a Y junction where the Boy Scout Trail turns northwest toward Indian Cove. Turn right onto the trail signed
for Willow Hole, and commence travel northeast into a
narrowing valley bounded by increasingly impressive rock
formations.

After 1.2 miles (1.9 km) through this narrowing valley, the trail disintegrates into a wide sandy wash that twists through the Wonderland before bottoming out at Willow Hole. Although the Joshua trees will have mostly disappeared by this point, a surprising amount of vegetation, including California juniper, single-leaf pinyon pine, and scrub oak, will continue to remind you that you're traveling through the high desert.

While the wash is well defined enough that it shouldn't pose a navigational risk, be aware that several smaller washes join from the north and south. A wrong turn up one of these washes could lead to some anxious detours. If you maintain your focus on the main wash, which widens appreciably as you get closer to Willow Hole, you should have no trouble keeping to the correct path.

At 3.3 miles (5.3 km), the wash makes a conspicuous S bend through some of the most impressive formations thus far. The wash straightens out to approach a grove of willows in a swale ringed by towering rock piles—the eponymous "willow hole." The lowest points of this swale can fill up with water during wetter times. These small pools provide an important water supply for the Wonderland's population of bighorn sheep. The importance of this area to the endangered bighorns is a key reason why the park closes Willow Hole to backpackers. Day hikers may enjoy the countless nooks, crannies, and casual scrambles surrounding Willow Hole for several happy hours, but be sure to turn back before dark to avoid any confusion as you navigate out of the Wonderland.

LOST HORSE VALLEY

When most people think of Joshua Tree, Lost Horse Valley, with its Joshua tree forests and towering granite formations, is the first place that comes to mind. Lost Horse Valley runs roughly north to south from the southern reaches of the Wonderland of Rocks to the windswept ridges along Lost Horse Mountain, and between the lofty heights of Quail Mountain in the west and Ryan Mountain on the east. Many of the park's most popular destinations and hiking trails lie within the confines of the valley, and accordingly, most of its human activity occurs here as well.

Several short nature trails and one thrilling cross-country exploration on the north end of the valley explore the Wonderland of Rocks and various man-made contrivances designed to facilitate mining and ranching operations. Other mining operations pepper Lost Horse Mountain, which swells toward Keys View, overlooking a sudden escarpment that melts into the vast Coachella Valley to the south.

The region features two popular campgrounds, Hidden Valley and Ryan, that offer limited campsites and thus fill up quickly. A third group campground sits upon Sheep Pass, which divides Lost Horse Valley from Queen Valley to the east. This region also features two picnic areas at Hidden Valley and Cap Rock, which cater to families looking to enjoy the desert at a more leisurely pace.

In addition to containing many prime hiking destinations, Lost Horse Valley is also the epicenter of rock climbing in

OPPOSITE *Post-dawn reflections at Barker Dam (Route 13)*

Joshua Tree. At any given boulder pile, in areas like Hemingway, Hidden Valley, Hall of Horrors, and the Oyster Bar, you will undoubtedly see climbers testing their skills and mettle on world-famous routes. Although not technically hikes, the informal trails around these landmarks, including a hike described in Route 20, are fine places for unstructured wandering.

12 HIDDEN VALLEY NATURE TRAIL

Distance: 1 mile (1.6 km)
Elevation gain: 150 feet (45 m)
High point: 4269 feet (1301 m)
Difficulty: Easy
Trail surface: Sand and occasional rock outcrops and staircases
Map: USGS 7.5-minute Indian Cove
GPS: 34.012413° N, -116.167941° W
Notes: Day use only; good for kids; interpretive trail; pit toilets and picnic area at trailhead; historical interest

> This easy, don't-miss hike through a beautiful hidden valley presents a perfect introduction to all of the things that make Joshua Tree great: high-desert vegetation, evocative granite formations, and a dash of local history. Kids will love the countless nooks and crannies to explore, and adults will bask in the beauty of the place.

GETTING THERE
Driving: From the park's West Entrance, south of the town of Joshua Tree, drive southeast on Park Boulevard for 8.9 miles (14.3 km) to the junction at Intersection Rock. Turn right toward the Hidden Valley picnic area, and park in the large lot adjacent to the trailhead.

Who left their recliner on the rock pile?

Transit: The RoadRunner Shuttle between the town of Joshua Tree and Hidden Valley runs every two hours. The more frequent interpark shuttle between Barker Dam and Jumbo Rocks stops at Hidden Valley every thirty minutes.

ON THE TRAIL

The routefinding on this short loop is simple. From the trailhead, ascend on a well-traveled path to a gap between two large outcrops standing sentinel over the entrance of the valley. Once past this gap, you reach a junction with the Hidden Valley Nature Trail loop that runs in an oblong circle through the center of the valley. Turn left to begin a mellow

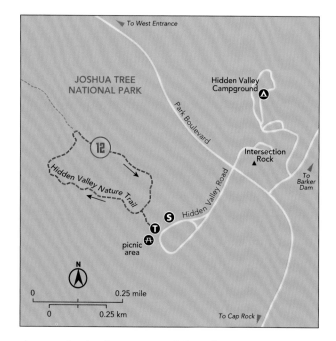

descent that leads west toward the valley's primary wash at 0.45 mile (0.7 km). The trail bends right to remain in the wash for a short distance and then continues right onto the well-marked trail to continue on an equally mellow incline back to the trailhead. Occasional climber's trails present possible side paths along the way.

Simple though the navigation is, you will find a lot to explore and admire along the way. Interpretive panels describe the valley's history and natural environment. Impressive specimens of single-leaf pinyon pine and Muller oak eke out a marginal existence by finding water-retaining pockets within cracks in the granite, giving the valley a surprisingly lush appearance despite its location in an arid region. The area's ubiquitous monzogranite formations put an exclamation point on the scenery with countless fascinating features.

13 BARKER DAM

Distance: 1.3 miles (2.1 km)
Elevation gain: 115 feet (35 m)
High point: 4295 feet (1310 m)
Difficulty: Easy
Trail surface: Hard-packed sand
Map: USGS 7.5-minute Indian Cove
GPS: 34.024282° N, -116.141971° W
Notes: Day use only; good for kids; pit toilets at trailhead; historical interest

> This quintessential Joshua Tree experience focuses on one of the rarest spectacles the park can offer: a standing body of water. For decades, the Barker Dam has captured runoff coursing through the Wonderland of Rocks within a wide basin. The reservoir often dries up during the summer, but even a modest amount of water creates a beautiful scene with granite rock piles reflected in its still surface. Although the reservoir once hydrated thirsty cattle, today it is a vital water source for the Wonderland's resident herd of bighorn sheep.

Watch for bighorn sheep around Barker Dam reservoir.

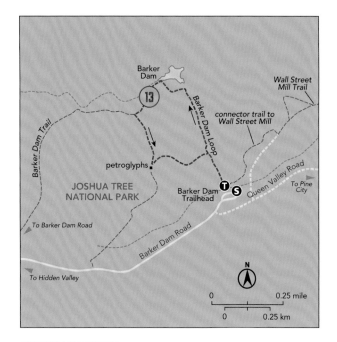

GETTING THERE

Driving: From the park's West Entrance, south of the town of Joshua Tree, drive southeast on Park Boulevard for 8.9 miles (14.3 km) to the junction at Intersection Rock. Turn left onto Barker Dam Road and follow it for 1.5 miles (2.4 km) to the Barker Dam parking area.

Transit: The RoadRunner Shuttle between the West Entrance Visitor Center and Barker Dam runs every two hours. The more frequent interpark shuttle between Barker Dam and Jumbo Rocks stops at Barker Dam every thirty minutes.

ON THE TRAIL

Visitors should be prepared for the possibility that there may not be any water in the reservoir. During California's historic 2012–2016 drought, the reservoir was perpetually empty, but during wet years like 2011 and 2017, the dam was full to the brim. A quick look at recent rainfall in the Southern California region will offer a hint as to whether you can expect water, as will a call to a visitor center. Even if there isn't any water, the surrounding scenery as well as the prehistory and recent history on display make this hike worth your while.

From the parking area, head north on the well-traveled trail. Continue straight at a junction with the return section of the loop, and follow the trail through a cool stretch of canyon before reaching a spacious basin at 0.4 mile (0.6 km). Within this basin, a large body of water held by Barker Dam may or may not shimmer in the high-desert sun. If there is water, consider getting here around dawn for a chance to spy bighorn sheep on the opposite banks of the reservoir. Your odds of seeing them at this time are better, since they're more active in the morning, and there's less noise from other visitors.

The trail bends to the left to skirt the southern banks of the reservoir. At 0.5 mile (0.8 km), you reach the dam itself. The dam was the target for an overwhelming amount of graffiti in past years, but recent projects have helped to restore it to its former desert chic glory. Continue on a descent past the dam into a small valley dotted with Joshua trees and California junipers. Keep left at a junction with a trail leading west toward Barker Dam Road at 0.7 mile (1.1 km), and continue south to another junction with a connector trail at 0.9 mile (1.4 km) leading to Hidden Valley Campground. Turn right and walk a short distance down this connector trail to reach a beautiful petroglyph panel carved by the desert's indigenous inhabitants on an overhanging rock wall.

After admiring the petroglyphs, backtrack to the previous junction, and turn right to return to the parking area via a short walk that runs through a gap in the granite formations bounding the southwestern corner of the valley. At 1.1 miles (1.8 km), you will reach the initial stretch of trail that led you to the dam. Turn right here for an easy 0.2-mile (0.3 km) walk back to the car.

GOING FARTHER

You can attach the routes into the Wonderland of Rocks (Route 14) and Wall Street Mill (Route 15) by way of a 0.35-mile (0.55 km) connector trail that runs west to east between the Barker Dam parking area and the Wall Street Mill Trailhead.

14   WONDERLAND OF ROCKS

Distance: 3.6 miles (5.8 km)
Elevation gain: 250 feet (75 m)
High point: 4528 feet (1380 m)
Difficulty: Challenging
Trail surface: Soft sand in the washes and occasional passages across exposed granite
Map: USGS 7.5-minute Indian Cove
GPS: 34.028127° N, -116.138651° W
Notes: Routefinding and navigation required; day use only; moderate terrain and light scrambling; pit toilets at trailhead

The Wonderland of Rocks comprises a vast, seemingly impenetrable granite maze carved into countless fascinating formations. Most of the routes that explore the Wonderland do so on the margins, which prevents hikers from inadvertently wandering into the area and becoming lost. Although most of the Wonderland lies outside the scope of this book as well as the navigational ability of most hikers, this delightful out-and-back route allows hikers with sufficient navigational skill an opportunity to explore the interior of this memorable place.

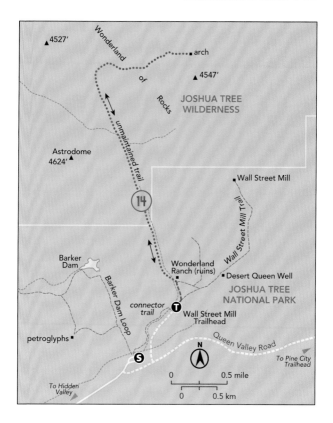

GETTING THERE

Driving: From the park's West Entrance, south of the town of Joshua Tree, drive southeast on Park Boulevard for 8.9 miles (14.3 km) to the junction at Intersection Rock. Turn left onto Barker Dam Road and follow it for 1.5 miles (2.4 km) to a junction with Queen Valley Road just before the Barker Dam parking area. After a little over 0.1 mile (0.2 km) on Queen Valley Road, turn left onto the road signed for the Wall Street Mill Trail.

Transit: The RoadRunner Shuttle between the West Entrance Visitor Center and Barker Dam runs every two hours. The more frequent interpark shuttle between Barker Dam and Jumbo Rocks stops at Barker Dam every thirty minutes. From Barker Dam, you can follow an extension of the Barker Dam Loop trail east for 0.35 mile (0.6 km) to the Wall Street Mill Trailhead.

ON THE TRAIL

Before starting out, please note that you will need to have and be able to read a topographic map and use a compass to orient yourself. These directions refer to prominent landmarks on the topo, and without a detailed map and compass, you run the risk of getting lost. Do not attempt this hike unless you have sufficient navigational skill.

Set out on the Wall Street Mill Trail, and turn left after 100 yards (90 m). This path leads you to the ruins of Wonderland Ranch's crumbling walls. Not much is known about the Ohlson family who built the ranch, aside from the fact that they came here lured by the promise of gold and left behind hints of a passion for pink architecture. In addition to the ruins, you may also find a small dam and reservoir upstream within a prominent wash to the west.

Pick up an informal trail leading west through a tangle of oaks that soon turns north and straightens out within a wash. This wash, informally known as Wonderland Wash, runs north-northwest into the heart of the Wonderland of Rocks. As you travel through the wash, you'll encounter disjointed informal trails that circumvent minor obstacles, as well as a few stretches of light scrambling over granite outcrops. There's just enough challenge thanks to the scrambling to keep things interesting and fun without travel becoming dangerous.

The wash peters out at 0.8 mile (1.3 km) within a spacious valley bounded by towering formations. At this point, you aren't too deep into the Wonderland, and the wash you

Playing peekaboo with a Muller oak

came in on offers a quick and easy return to the certainty of established trails. This is a good spot to simply wander around and explore the countless nooks and crannies. It is also an ideal turnaround spot if you're less confident about your navigational skills.

If you're itching for more, continue heading north-northwest along informal paths connecting patches of granitic bedrock. Before you go too far, look west and spot a massive rounded dome (peak 4624 on the topo), the largest unbroken block of granite in sight. This landmark, informally known as the Astrodome, is a good landmark to help you remain oriented.

At about 1 mile (1.6 km), cross a prominent wash and then continue in the same north-northwest direction along informal paths. At 1.3 miles (2.1 km), you will reach a large basin opening up to the east (your right) that lies about a quarter mile southeast of peak 4527. Turn right into this basin, but keep to the southern margins to find a gap that continues east into a second basin. Another informal path threads through the center of this basin to a prominent rocky outcrop located just north of peak 4547 on your topo map. Here, you can reach an impressive rock arch by way of a short, steep scramble.

The arch marks the end of the route. Carefully work your way back west through the connected basins, and turn south to return to the wash you came in on.

15 WALL STREET MILL

Distance: 1.5 miles (2.4 km)
Elevation gain: 100 feet (30 m)
High point: 4351 feet (1326 m)
Difficulty: Easy
Trail surface: Wide, sandy former dirt trail
Map: USGS 7.5-minute Indian Cove
GPS: 34.028127° N, -116.138651° W
Notes: Day use only; good for kids; pit toilets at trailhead; historical interest

With dozens of workers digging up ore from mines on the east side of Queen Valley from the early 1890s and all the way

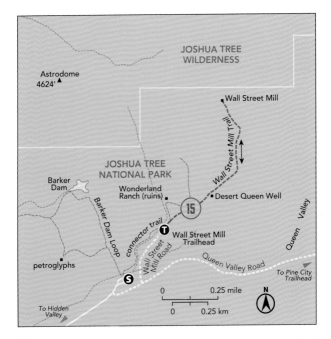

into the 1960s, mine owners needed a place to process all of their findings into something that they could sell. Bill Keys's mill on the southeast end of the Wonderland of Rocks filled that purpose for decades, from the time Keys established the mill until he went to prison for murdering Worth Bagley. Hikers can visit the ruins of the mill, along with several other mining curiosities and a few automotive reclamation projects on this easy stroll.

GETTING THERE

Driving: From the park's West Entrance south of Joshua Tree, drive southeast on Park Boulevard for 8.9 miles (14.3 km) to the junction at Intersection Rock. Turn left onto Barker Dam

The Wall Street Mill

Road and follow it for 1.5 miles (2.4 km) to a junction with Queen Valley Road just before the Barker Dam parking area. After a little over 0.1 mile (0.2 km) on Queen Valley Road, turn left onto the road signed for the Wall Street Mill Trail.

Transit: The RoadRunner Shuttle between the West Entrance Visitor Center and Barker Dam runs every two hours. The more frequent interpark shuttle between Barker Dam and Jumbo Rocks stops at Barker Dam every thirty minutes. From Barker Dam, you can follow an extension of the Barker

Dam Loop trail east for 0.3 mile (0.5 km) to the Wall Street Mill Trailhead.

ON THE TRAIL

Find the trailhead just left of the restrooms, and commence an easy, but often sandy stroll along the old road leading to the mill. After only 100 yards (90 m) or so, you reach a junction with a road leading north toward the ruins of Wonderland Ranch and providing access to the Wonderland of Rocks (see Route 14). Make a short stop at the Wonderland Ranch ruins for an additional 0.1 mile (0.2 km) of walking, or continue walking northeast. As you progress, keep your eyes peeled for the rusted-out hulk of an ancient car tucked into the bushes north of the trail at around 0.15 mile (0.24 km).

After passing a windmill and some rusted detritus marking the site of the Desert Queen Well at 0.3 mile (0.5 km), the trail bends to the north through increasingly dense vegetation. At 0.7 mile (1.1 km), an informal path splits from the main trail and leads toward the mill. The mill is fenced off and marked with no trespassing signs, but that won't prevent some casual exploration of the area surrounding it. You'll find another rusted-out car that may need a little engine work before you can get it running again.

In addition to the historical interest of the mill itself, hikers may also enjoy some casual exploration around the margins of the Wonderland of Rocks. One prominent wash draining the west slope of Queen Mountain drains into a cove just north of the mill, affording a number of spots for casual scrambling and picnicking.

Whatever your intentions are for exploring the area, be sure to leave everything as you found it. This area in particular has suffered under the onslaught of vandalism, including the toppling of an old stone marker that Bill Keys set up to commemorate his murder of Worth Bagley.

16 CAP ROCK NATURE TRAIL

Distance: 0.4 mile (0.6 km)
Elevation gain: Negligible
High point: 4268 feet (1301 m)
Difficulty: Easy
Trail surface: Smooth, hard-packed sand
Map: USGS 7.5-minute Keys View
GPS: 33.989204° N, -116.163529° W
Notes: Day use only; interpretive trail; good for kids; pit toilets at trailhead

If you're wondering to yourself, "Where should I take my children in Joshua Tree?" consider the Cap Rock Nature Trail. Just about anybody can hike this easy route; plus there are

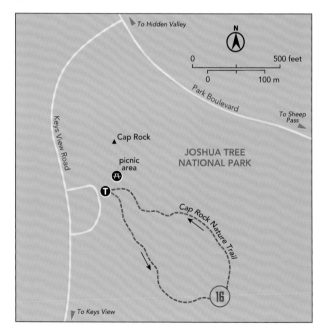

Dusk evokes serenity in the Joshua tree forest.

picnic tables in the shade of a massive boulder pile capped by a large rock where kids can frolic and explore to their hearts' content. Adults will enjoy the scenery, and everybody will learn something about desert foliage thanks to the regularly spaced interpretive panels along the way.

GETTING THERE

From the park's West Entrance, south of the town of Joshua Tree, follow Park Boulevard southeast for 10.5 miles (16.9 km) to a junction with Keys View Road. Turn right onto Keys View Road, and then make a left turn into the Cap Rock picnic area parking lot after 0.2 mile (0.3 km).

ON THE TRAIL

From the east side of the parking lot, find the wide, smooth trail adjacent to the pit toilets. The trail immediately reaches a Y junction. Turn right to follow the southern branch as it passes between two large, picturesque boulder piles. Interpretive plaques placed every 100 to 200 feet (30 to 60 m) detail the various plant species on display along the trail, including evocative-sounding names like Mormon tea (ephedra) or desert almond. A dense Joshua tree forest closes in along the trail, casting long shadows during crepuscular light.

After the trail turns back toward the trailhead at 0.2 mile (0.3 km), it passes through a narrow gap in the rocks before heading straight back to Cap Rock's parking and picnic areas.

17 LOST HORSE MINE

Distance: 6.7 miles (10.8 km)
Elevation gain: 1000 feet (305 m)
High point: 5113 feet (1558 m)
Difficulty: Challenging
Trail surface: Wide dirt road to mine and narrow, sandy single-track for remainder of loop
Map: USGS 7.5-minute Keys View
GPS: 33.950717° N, -116.159853° W
Notes: Day use only; pit toilets at trailhead; historical interest

Joshua Tree's most productive and lucrative gold mine is the focal point for this extended trip through the highlands above Lost Horse Valley. In addition to the mine, hikers will also enjoy summit views from Lost Horse Mountain, equally spectacular views across Queen Valley from the east side of Lost Horse Mountain, several other mining relics scattered along the route, and a leisurely finish through Joshua tree woodland.

GETTING THERE
From the park's West Entrance, south of the town of Joshua Tree, follow Park Boulevard southeast for 10.5 miles

OPPOSITE *Come for the mine; stay for the views.*

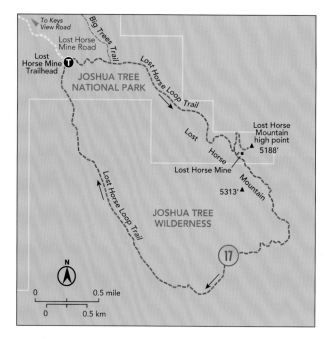

(16.9 km) to Keys View Road, and turn right. Continue south on Keys View Road for another 2.4 miles (3.9 km) to a junction with Lost Horse Mine Road, and turn left. Lost Horse Mine Road dead-ends at the trailhead after 1 mile (1.6 km).

ON THE TRAIL

Find the start of the trail just beyond a gate that closes Lost Horse Mine Road to vehicle traffic. You'll follow this dirt road on a moderate incline heading east. Stay straight at a junction with the Big Trees Trail that runs north to Ryan Ranch at 0.3 mile (0.5 km). The trail continues uphill through a broad valley before cresting a saddle at 1 mile (1.6 km) and passing a few mining claims just beyond. Once past this saddle, look north for good views of the voluptuous slopes of Ryan Mountain.

At 1.8 miles (2.9 km), the dirt road bends to the left to make a switchbacking approach to the mine; stop at the switchback to enjoy the view north across Ryan Mountain and Lost Horse Valley. After the switchback, the road reaches the ten-stamp mill and surrounding mine shafts associated with the Lost Horse Mine at 2.1 miles (3.4 km). The mill has been fenced off to curb vandalism, but you still get an up-close look at the elaborate contraption. Various mine shafts, long since closed off by the park, lie below the mill, with various bits of rusted-out equipment strewn about. Cables that used to pull ore up from these mines are still in evidence, and the size and scope of the site testify to how much activity once occurred here. A short scramble due east from the mine leads you to the summit of Lost Horse Mountain.

Many people turn back at the mine for a 4.2-mile (6.8 km) out-and-back hike. If you've got an appetite for more hiking, continue beyond the mine on a narrow trail that runs southeast toward a saddle between the Lost Horse Mountain high point and peak 5313. Just as the crowds magically thin out, you will find yourself commencing a steep, 325-foot (100 m) descent over 0.3 mile (0.5 km) that bottoms out at another set of mine shafts.

With the knee-smashing descent out of the way, settle in for a mildly undulating traverse along the eastern and southern slopes of Lost Horse Mountain. The trail passes numerous outcrops with outstanding views across Queen Valley that also serve as fine spots to enjoy a quiet break. At 3.2 miles (5.1 km), you reach another mine and the remnants of an old cabin belonging to a long-forgotten prospector.

You face one final climb up and over another saddle before the trail settles into a gentle, extended descent through a valley studded with Joshua trees. This pleasant stretch of walking offers a generous dose of solitude relative to the busy section leading to the mine. This trail terminates at the west end of the Lost Horse Mine parking area.

18   INSPIRATION PEAK

Distance: 1.9 miles (3.1 km)
Elevation gain: 850 feet (260 m)
High point: 5578 feet (1700 m)
Difficulty: Moderate
Trail surface: Dirt with a few uneven rocky stretches
Map: USGS 7.5-minute Keys View
GPS: 33.927256° N, -116.187218° W
Notes: Informal trail marked by cairns in rough sections; minor navigation may be required; day use only; no restroom at trailhead

> Hundreds of park visitors travel to Keys View every day to take in the sweeping panorama surveying the Coachella Valley, the Salton Sea, and the distant San Jacinto and San Bernardino Mountains. Hikers who don't mind expending some extra effort can top those views with this moderate hike to Inspiration Peak, which takes in the Coachella Valley scenery as well as a large swath of Joshua Tree National Park itself.

GETTING THERE

From the park's West Entrance, follow Park Boulevard southeast for 10.5 miles (16.9 km) to a junction with Keys View Road. Turn right onto Keys View Road, and follow it 5.5 miles (8.9 km) south until it dead-ends at the Keys View parking area. The unassuming, unmarked trail lies on the northwest side of the parking area. If you're having trouble locating the path, count three parking spots to the right from the handicapped parking spot, and there's your trail.

ON THE TRAIL

After finding the unmarked trailhead, begin a brisk climb heading north along an informal, but easily followed trail that gains 325 feet (100 m) in a mere 0.3 mile (0.5 km). This

Taking inspiration from the rising sun over Lost Horse Valley

initial climb tops out at the first of three summits, and after catching your breath, you can admire the fine views in all directions. If the stiff climb saps your interest in going all the way to Inspiration Peak, you can stop here and still enjoy a considerable scenic improvement over that of Keys View.

As you look toward the next summit, peak 5558 only a quarter mile to the west, you face that dispiriting experience of losing 100 feet (30 m) of elevation only to have to regain it plus some interest. When you reach peak 5558, you can follow a short informal trail that splits off on the left to the rocky summit. If you feel satisfied, you can always turn around at this summit.

Beyond peak 5558, continue northwest and negotiate a rocky section marked by cairns on a short descent along a

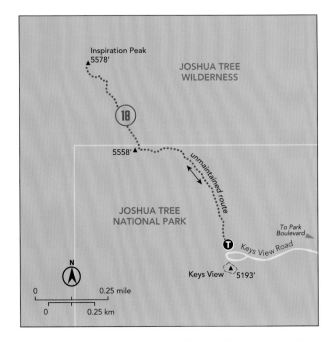

ridge leading to Inspiration Peak. Reach Inspiration Peak after 0.9 mile (1.4 km), and from here, you can enjoy the views that live up to the peak's auspicious name. For even better views north into the interior of the park, follow a short path leading northeast to the northern edge of the summit block.

The combination of a large, flat peak and the stunning views in all directions make Inspiration Peak a great place to linger and relax. Adventurous hikers armed with headlamps and extra layers of warm clothing will enjoy this hike either pre-sunrise or pre-sunset. Joshua Tree's gorgeous sunrises and sunsets only improve as you gain elevation, and this is one of the most accessible places to enjoy that particular spectacle. Hold on to your hats, though; winter and spring winds can blow fiercely here.

19 RYAN RANCH

Distance: 1.1 miles (1.8 km)
Elevation gain: 90 feet (30 m)
High point: 4368 feet (1331 m)
Difficulty: Easy
Trail surface: A sandy dirt road
Map: USGS 7.5-minute Keys View
GPS: 33.989307° N, -116.155079° W
Notes: Day use only; good for kids; pit toilets at trailhead; historical interest

> This short, family-friendly hike visits the ruins of Ryan Ranch, the site of J. D. Ryan's homestead built alongside a spring that also supplied water to the nearby Lost Horse Mine. Fine views west and north across Lost Horse Valley combine with picturesque boulder piles closer afoot to make this a short but satisfying stroll.

The foundation needs work, but you can't beat the location.

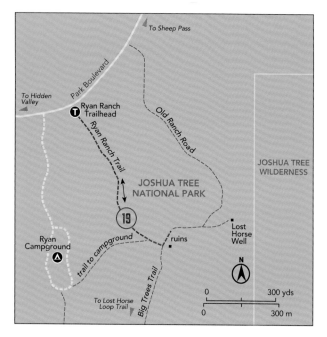

GETTING THERE

From the park's West Entrance, drive southeast on Park Boulevard for 11.1 miles (17.9 km) to the signed Ryan Ranch trailhead on the right (east) side of the road.

ON THE TRAIL

From the parking area, step onto the wide, sandy dirt road and follow it southeast on a barely perceptible incline. The road approaches but doesn't quite reach a picturesque pile of boulders with a large slab standing upright. As you pass this rock pile, the ranch road bends left to make a short climb up to the ruins of the ranch house.

Only the foundation and adobe walls of the main structure remain standing following a 1978 fire that swept the ranch. In addition to the main structure, a handful of other structures, along with the Lost Horse Well, still stand to the west of the main house. You can reach all of these structures via informal trails that radiate from the main house.

The hour before sunset is a great time to take this hike. Late-afternoon light washes over the valley's countless Joshua trees, casting long shadows and throwing the surrounding geography into sharp relief.

GOING FARTHER

The remnants of an old road that the original occupants used to reach the Lost Horse Mine leads south past a junction with the California Riding and Hiking Trail. At the junction, the old road becomes the Big Trees Trail. For an ambitious hike, you could follow this trail to Lost Horse Mine and back for a 9-mile (14.5 km) roundtrip with 1100 feet (335 m) of elevation gain.

20 HALL OF HORRORS

Distance: 1.1 miles (1.8 km)
Elevation gain: 70 feet (20 m)
High point: 4341 feet (1323 m)
Difficulty: Easy
Trail surface: Hard-packed sand
Map: USGS 7.5-minute Keys View
GPS: 33.998483° N, -116.145066° W
Notes: Day use only; good for kids; informal trails; pit toilets at trailhead

Although the Hall of Horrors is better known as a rock-climbing destination, the semiformal network of trails encircling the formations also doubles as a nice spot for a leisurely hike. While exploring the area, you can admire the grotesque forms of the surrounding boulder piles on your way to a secluded rock arch halfway through this prescribed loop hike.

GETTING THERE

From the park's West Entrance, south of the town of Joshua Tree, follow Park Boulevard southeast for 12 miles (19.3 km) to the Hall of Horrors parking area on the west side of the road.

ON THE TRAIL

The trailhead offers you two options where the trail immediately branches. Revegetation projects surrounding the beginning of the trail testify to the need to remain on the established trails. Keep right and follow the fenced trail, which soon becomes an informal, foot-traffic-maintained path. Stay on this path as it veers to the right of the two largest rock piles.

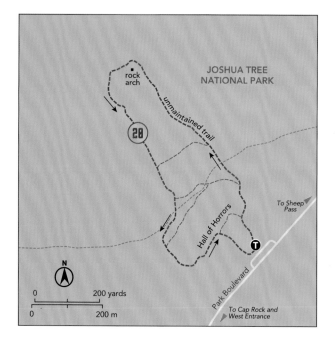

A hidden arch near the Hall of Horrors

Once you clear the two main rock piles comprising the Hall of Horrors, the trail reaches open desert. From this point, you should see a smaller boulder pile standing all by its lonesome 0.2 mile (0.3 km) ahead. Approach that boulder pile and follow an informal trail to wrap around the back. Tucked into a deep crease on the north side of the boulder pile, look for an arch. You'll get your best view of the arch by scrambling up a steep, slanting slab within the crease.

To return, loop around to the other side of the arch rock pile, and follow another informal trail back to the Hall of Horrors. Be sure to veer left to walk between the two largest rock piles at 1 mile (1.6 km) or else you risk going off course and having to traipse through vegetation to find your way back.

21 RYAN MOUNTAIN

Distance: 2.8 miles (4.5 km)
Elevation gain: 1050 feet (320 m)
High point: 5457 feet (1663 m)
Difficulty: Moderate
Trail surface: Dirt single-track punctuated with rocky spots
Map: USGS 7.5-minute Keys View
GPS: 34.003248° N, -116.136306° W
Notes: Day use only; pit toilets at trailhead

> With one of the few formal trails leading to a peak within the park, Ryan Mountain receives quite a bit of traffic from hikers seeking sweeping summit views in all directions. This steep, no-nonsense climb brings you to the summit in a hurry, where you can enjoy impressive views in all directions.

GETTING THERE

Driving: From the park's West Entrance, south of the town of Joshua Tree, drive southeast on Park Boulevard for 12.6 miles (20.3 km) to the Ryan Mountain Trailhead.

Transit: The RoadRunner Shuttle from the town of Joshua Tree to Jumbo Rocks stops at the Ryan Mountain Trailhead every two hours. The more frequent interpark shuttle from Barker Dam to Jumbo Rocks stops at the trailhead every thirty minutes.

ON THE TRAIL

Step onto the Ryan Mountain Trail and follow it south as it threads its way through two large boulder piles. After 0.2 mile (0.3 km), you reach a junction with the Sheep Pass Connector Trail that runs east toward Sheep Pass Group Campground. Keep right at this junction and continue on the

OPPOSITE *Rainbow over Hall of Horrors viewed from Ryan Mountain Trail*

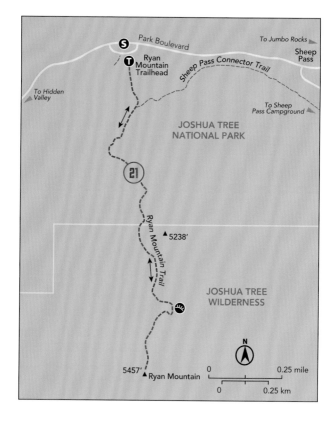

trail as it makes a steep, oblique climb up the mountain's western slope toward a saddle between the summit and peak 5238.

At 1.1 miles (1.8 km), the trail reaches a vista point that overlooks Queen Valley for a quick teaser of the full summit view. From the vista point, finish the summit approach with a 0.3-mile (0.5 km) climb that tops out at a rock pile crowning the spacious peak.

Sharp-eyed hikers armed with a map of the park will be able to pick out a number of prominent landmarks. Look west to see Quail Mountain, the park's high point rising from the western edge of Lost Horse Valley. The pale, rugged reaches of the Wonderland of Rocks lie to the north and extend east to an abrupt geologic transition west of Queen Mountain. Queen Valley dominates the eastern landscape, and you can easily pick out volcanic Malapai Hill rising from the center. Southern California's towering twin high points, Mount San Jacinto and Mount San Gorgonio, rise high above the Little San Bernardinos to the south and west.

QUEEN VALLEY

Travel east from Lost Horse Valley and cross Sheep Pass, and you'll enter a second, larger valley known as Queen Valley. Queen Valley runs from its northern boundary at Queen Mountain south to the highlands of the Little San Bernardinos. The valley is bound on the west by Ryan and Lost Horse Mountains and to the east by the Hexie Mountains. Like Lost Horse Valley, Queen Valley also contains thriving Joshua tree forests, and its margins are lined by monzogranite boulder piles that feature some of the park's most popular hiking. Park Boulevard divides the northern third of the valley from the southern two-thirds, and the progressively bumpy dirt Geology Tour Road provides access to the southern reaches of the valley.

Each route in this chapter lies north of Park Boulevard within the upper third of Queen Valley. Aside from a rocky, challenging summit approach to Queen Mountain, these hikes either explore the northeastern edge of the valley, where historic mining sites mingle with splendid vistas, or the eastern margins around the popular Jumbo Rocks area. Here a trio of shorter nature trails tour impressive boulder formations along with the park's largest campground.

OPPOSITE *Pinnacles and spires on the Split Rock Trail (Route 28)*

22 QUEEN MOUNTAIN

Distance: 4 miles (6.4 km)
Elevation gain: 1200 feet (365 m)
High point: 5682 feet (1732 m)
Difficulty: Strenuous
Trail surface: Open desert and steep, rocky slopes
Map: USGS 7.5-minute Queen Mountain
GPS: 34.034867° N, -116.107656° W
Notes: Day use only; navigation required; difficult terrain

> Presiding over her namesake valley like the monarch she is, Queen Mountain beckons far and wide to ambitious peak baggers. And like any royalty, she demands tribute. In this case, that tribute comes in the form of a challenging scramble up a rocky slope and through a narrow ravine before you can admire the exceptional views from the twin summit blocks crowning the peak.

GETTING THERE

From the North Entrance Station, south of Twentynine Palms, drive south on Park Boulevard for 4.5 miles (7.2 km) to Pinto Wye, and keep right to stay on Park Boulevard. After another 5.8 miles (9.3 km) on Park Boulevard, turn right onto Bighorn Pass Road (smooth dirt, suitable for low-clearance vehicles). After 0.4 mile (0.6 km), turn right onto unsigned O'Dell Road (smooth dirt, suitable for low-clearance vehicles), and follow it for 1.5 miles (2.4 km) until it ends at a turnout. This turnout is your starting point.

ON THE TRAIL

Before getting started, please note that this route requires off-trail navigation. These directions refer to physical land-marks represented on topographic maps. Do not attempt this route unless you are adept at using a map and compass

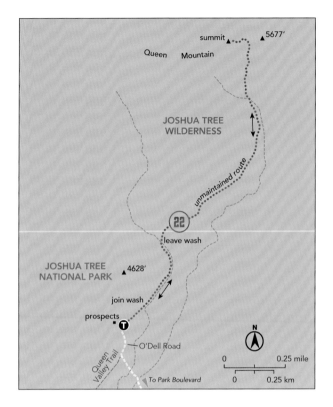

for routefinding and have both a topographic map and a compass in hand.

From the turnout, head northeast in the direction of a wash that runs south to north past the east slope of peak 4628. You reach this wash after just over 0.1 mile (0.2 km) of walking, and it provides a nice avenue to follow for the next 0.3 mile (0.5 km). At 0.5 mile (0.8 km), leave the wash and head northeast toward the steep ridge forming the southern flank of Queen Mountain. As you peer up at the mountain's twin summits, commit the gap between the two peaks to

Early birds always get the best light over Queen Valley.

memory. This gap will be your target as you make the final summit approach.

Continue across open desert toward the eastern slope of Queen Mountain's southern ridge. At 1.2 miles (1.9 km), just before a steep wash, turn left to head directly up the rocky slope. Cairns mark the route here and there, but they blend in so seamlessly with the terrain that they are often difficult to follow. If you can't keep to the cairns, continue climbing the slope parallel to the wash until you reach the 5160-foot contour. At this point, cut across the wash and continue the steep climb through a broad rocky ravine that runs due north directly toward the gap between the summits.

At 1.8 miles (2.9 km), this rocky ravine flattens out at the gap between the summits, and you can begin the final push to the top. You have two choices regarding which peak you top out on. The western peak is the higher point, but the eastern peak contains the actual benchmark. Your best bet for the western peak is to wrap around it and approach from the north so as to avoid some rocky shelves.

From the top, you have unparalleled views south into expansive Queen Valley as it descends toward Pleasant Valley and the Little San Bernardino Mountains. Views southwest and west pick up familiar landmarks visible from most Joshua Tree high points, including Mount San Jacinto and Mount San Gorgonio. Closer at hand, you should be able to pick out Ryan Mountain on the west side of Queen Valley, and beyond that, the rounded form of Quail Mountain punctuating the skyline.

The return trip follows the same course, but you can expect to take a slightly different path back owing to the lack of trail. Please avoid adding cairns to the route as they may confuse future hikers. Also, exercise caution on the downhills. It may seem like a relief that gravity is your friend again, but your knees will thank you later for taking a patient, deliberate approach.

23 PINE CITY

Distance: 4 miles (6.4 km)
Elevation gain: 230 feet (70 m)
High point: 4575 feet (1395 m)
Difficulty: Moderate
Trail surface: Wide dirt road with a short section of sandy wash
Map: USGS 7.5-minute Queen Mountain
GPS: 34.023392° N, -116.077680° W
Notes: Day use only; good for kids; pit toilets at trailhead; backcountry registration board at trailhead; historical interest

This pleasant stroll traverses Joshua tree woodland in the northeast corner of Queen Valley to reach an old mining claim, an overlook that takes in a rugged canyon, and the titular Pine City. This curiously named landmark consists of

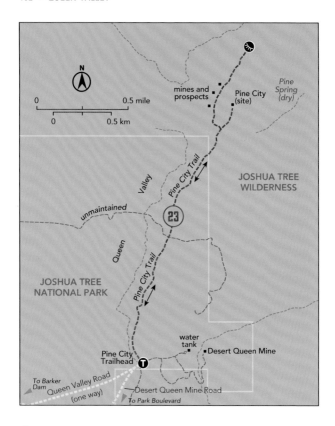

numerous boulder piles and some rather impressive Muller oaks and, of course, pinyon pines. Although the exact origins of its name are unclear, there's no denying that this sheltered garden of boulders and pinyons is an intriguing spot.

GETTING THERE

From the North Entrance Station, south of Twentynine Palms, drive south on Park Boulevard for 4.5 miles (7.2 km) to Pinto Wye, and keep right to stay on Park Boulevard. After another 5.1 miles (8.2 km), turn right onto unpaved Desert

Desert habitats juxtapose nicely with snowcapped mountains.

Queen Mine Road (safe for low-clearance vehicles) and drive 1.4 miles (2.3 km) to the Pine City Trailhead.

ON THE TRAIL

From the combined trailhead for the Pine City, Desert Queen Mine, and Lucky Boy Loop Trails, head north on the wide former mining road on an undulating ascent. Sparse Joshua tree forest and nice views toward Queen Mountain to the northwest are the primary highlights along the way, although the walk itself is quite relaxing. At 0.75 mile (1.2 km), you'll pass a vague, unmarked junction with an old roadbed that crosses Queen Valley and connects with a set of mining claims at the start of the Queen Mountain route (see Route 22).

From that junction, the trail continues in the same manner until it reaches junctions with some obscure paths leading west from the main road. The topo maps show these paths leading toward the site of an old cistern that collected water at a spring, but you may have a difficult time finding and keeping to them. After cresting a ridge at 1.4 miles (2.3 km), the road reaches a junction where the main path turns left and an informal trail continues straight toward the Pine City site.

Head straight to reach the heart of Pine City. Rumor has it that this spacious flat bounded by granite boulder piles once housed the structures associated with the nearby mines, but no trace of that remains today. What you will find is a beautiful glade rimmed by boulders and graced by numerous pinyon pines. You can wander around this area to your heart's content, perhaps scrambling onto some appealing boulders or lounging in the luxurious (at least for the desert) shade of a large pinyon pine.

Back on the main trail, follow the road onto a low ridge above Pine City as it continues north past a set of abandoned mine shafts. The road then terminates at the base of a low hill. This spot peers into the deep, rugged canyon that drains the southwest slopes of Queen Mountain and disintegrates into a sandy wash just south of the Contact Mine Trail (Route 32).

24 DESERT QUEEN MINE

Distance: 1.5 miles (2.4 km)
Elevation gain: 300 feet (90 m)
High point: 4462 feet (1360 m)
Difficulty: Moderate
Trail surface: Rocky former mining roads and a sandy wash
Map: USGS 7.5-minute Queen Mountain
GPS: 34.023392° N, -116.077680° W
Notes: Day use only; good for kids; pit toilets at trailhead; backcountry registration board at trailhead, historical interest

Although it never matched the more successful Lost Horse Mine in gold production, the Desert Queen Mine operated for sixty-seven years and was one of the more productive mines in the region. Rich with the sort of lascivious history that would fill tabloids today, the numerous mine shafts and

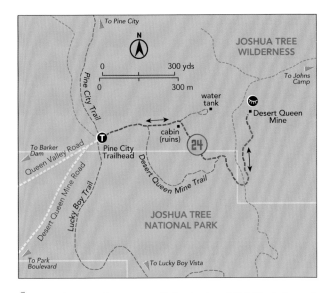

rusted-out equipment recall the lawless Wild West days of the park before its formal protection.

GETTING THERE

From the North Entrance Station, south of Twentynine Palms, drive south on Park Boulevard for 4.5 miles (7.2 km) to Pinto Wye, and keep right to stay on Park Boulevard. After another 5.1 miles (8.2 km), turn right onto unpaved Desert Queen Mine Road (safe for low-clearance vehicles) and drive 1.4 miles (2.3 km) to the Pine City Trailhead.

ON THE TRAIL

From the combined trailhead for the Pine City, Lucky Boy Loop, and Desert Queen Mine Trails, head east on the old mining road that once serviced the mine. At 0.1 mile (0.2 km), turn right to remain on this road. Continuing straight leads you to a water tank on the edge of the cliff for some nice views. Shortly after the right turn, you reach the

You can explore the first 10–15 feet (3–5 m) of the Desert Queen Mine.

remains of an old cabin at 0.2 mile (0.3 km) whose walls are still mostly intact.

After the cabin, the road begins to descend and deteriorate at the same time, creating a bumpy, cautious downhill walk that bottoms out within the wash at 0.3 mile (0.5 km). Cross over the wash to find a continuation of the road that leads uphill to the numerous shafts of the Desert Queen Mine from 0.4 to 0.55 mile (0.6 to 0.9 km). The mine, owned for a time by Bill Keys after being established by the notorious McHaney Gang, was a primary source of bullion for the nearby Wall Street Mill. Although never as productive as the Lost Horse Mine, this mine helped support Bill Keys and his family until Keys was convicted of manslaughter.

The trail reaches the last of the shafts atop a ridge over-looking the wash below as it gradually deepens into a canyon that drains out to open desert just southwest of Pinto Wye. Many of the minor shafts have collapsed either naturally or with the park's help, but some of the larger shafts are open for a distance of about 10 to 15 feet (3 to 5 m). You can't go any farther due to safety issues, but you can still get a bit of a thrill by peering into the darkness of these deep tunnels.

25 LUCKY BOY LOOP

Distance: 3.5 miles (5.6 km)
Elevation gain: 250 feet (75 m)
High point: 4525 feet (1379 m)
Difficulty: Moderate
Trail surface: Soft sand within network of washes, followed by firm dirt trail and stretch of road walking
Map: USGS 7.5-minute Queen Mountain
GPS: 34.017978° N, -116.082451° W
Notes: Day use only; good for kids; pit toilets at Pine City Trail-head; historical interest

The Lucky Boy Loop blends a nice mixture of features and experiences into a satisfying and compact package. The loop combines a trip to the site of the Elton Mine, which now doubles as a view-packed vista point overlooking the Jumbo Rocks and Pinto Basin areas. The return journey follows a meandering course through a granite wonderland graced with abundant pinyons and Muller oaks.

GETTING THERE
From the North Entrance Station, south of Twentynine Palms, drive south on Park Boulevard for 4.5 miles (7.2 km) to Pinto Wye, and keep right to stay on Park Boulevard. After

another 5.1 miles (8.2 km), turn right onto unpaved Desert Queen Mine Road (safe for low-clearance vehicles) and drive 0.9 mile (1.4 km) to the southern Lucky Boy Loop Trailhead. Note that this unassuming trailhead with space for a handful of cars is separate from the Pine City Trailhead.

ON THE TRAIL

Set out from the southern trailhead, heading generally southeast on a measured incline. You're following an old mining road used to reach the Elton Mine, but the passing years have let it revert to a narrower path. Hints of the granite wonderland to your north pop up here and there as you climb, but your goal for now is the Lucky Boy Vista at 1.2 miles (1.9 km). Keep straight at the junction with the northern branch of the Lucky Boy Loop Trail, and walk the

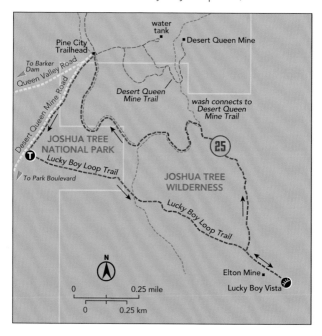

Lucky Boy Vista surveys the Split Rock Area and Pinto Basin.

last 0.2 mile (0.3 km) past the remnants of the Elton Mine to the vista spot. As vistas go, it's not the most jaw-dropping view you'll ever experience, but the higher perspective over the Jumbo Rocks area is still worth the effort.

For the northern half of the loop, backtrack to the junction and turn right. After a relatively mellow descent from the junction, the now sandy and somewhat rugged trail loses 100 feet (30 m) of elevation in the space of 0.1 mile (0.2 km) before bottoming out in the wash. Trekking poles will help you on this short stretch of rugged terrain.

After entering the wash, you reach a split where a tributary wash joins the main wash at 2 miles (3.2 km). Rather than keeping right to follow the main wash—which leads downhill toward the Desert Queen Mine—keep left to follow the tributary. This tributary winds through many interesting formations dotted with pinyon pines, California junipers, and Muller oaks, and there are a number of options for more leisurely exploration within the nooks and crannies.

The tributary wash reaches another split at 2.5 miles (4 km), and this time, take the right fork. This fork leads you to the Pine City Trailhead. When you reach the trailhead at 3 miles (4.8 km), turn left and follow the road for 0.5 mile (0.8 km) back to your car.

GOING FARTHER

If you turn right at the aforementioned wash at 2 miles (3.2 km), it leads you downhill to the Desert Queen Mine (see Route 24). You could then turn left to follow the old mining road uphill back to the Pine City Trailhead for a 4.2-mile (6.8 km) roundtrip hike.

26 SKULL ROCK NATURE TRAIL

Distance: 1.7 miles (2.7 km)
Elevation gain: 230 feet (70 m)
High point: 4369 feet (1332 m)
Difficulty: Easy
Trail surface: Mostly dirt with one long stretch following the road through Jumbo Rocks Campground
Maps: USGS 7.5-minute Queen Mountain, Malapai Hill
GPS: 33.997908° N, -116.060084° W
Notes: Day use only; interpretive trail; good for kids; pit toilets available within the campground

The Jumbo Rocks area features several popular anthropomorphic rock formations that fuel plenty of fascination and curiosity, but none do so quite as well as Skull Rock. The north face of this large oval boulder has cavities in all the right places and thus resembles a rather creepy-looking skull. The nature trail that begins and ends at the skull visits several other formations that, while not as instantly recognizable, are still among some of the most beautiful in the park.

GETTING THERE

Driving: From the North Entrance Station, south of Twentynine Palms, drive south on Park Boulevard for 4.5 miles (7.2 km) to Pinto Wye, and keep right to stay on Park Boulevard. Continue for 2.9 miles (4.7 km) to a pull-out directly

across from Skull Rock. The shared trailhead for Skull Rock Nature Trail and Discovery Nature Trail is on the north side of the road.

Transit: Three separate routes of the Road-Runner Shuttle terminate at Jumbo Rocks Campground. The Joshua Tree and Twentynine Palms shuttles arrive and depart every two hours; the more frequent interpark shuttle departs every thirty minutes. Note that if

You may find solitude at ever-popular Skull Rock early in the morning.

you take the shuttle, you will need to start this route from the western trailhead for Skull Rock Nature Trail, across from the entrance to Jumbo Rocks Campground, rather than the eastern trailhead across from Skull Rock itself.

ON THE TRAIL

From the roadside parking, step onto the combined Discovery Nature Trail and Skull Rock Nature Trail, and turn left immediately at the first junction. A second junction with the Discovery Nature Trail appears on the right after 0.15 mile (0.2 km) of travel heading west. Keep left again, and pass through a sandy wash separating two large parallel boulder piles. The trail continues on an incline until about the half-mile (0.8 km) mark at the shoulder of a vast granitic outcrop incised by crisscrossing joints.

The trail undulates along the southern end of this outcrop as it approaches Park Boulevard at 0.8 mile (1.3 km). This

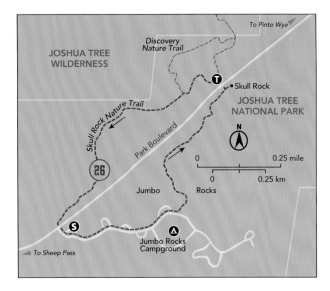

section of the road is often quite congested both with foot traffic and vehicle traffic, so exercise caution while crossing. Once on the other side, follow the paved access road through Jumbo Rocks Campground for 0.4 mile (0.6 km) before reaching the continuation of the trail on the eastern end of the campground.

The continuation of the trail climbs away from the campground, heading north toward Skull Rock. Along the way, look to the right for an unnamed, but recognizable rock formation sometimes colloquially referred to as "the Marbles" that has been the subject of much photographic study. Several interpretive plaques along the way also highlight some of the local vegetation.

Just before the trail reaches its conclusion at Park Boulevard, a short path leads to Skull Rock. To say Skull Rock is a popular spot is a bit of an understatement. Unless you come early in the morning, you can expect to share the spot with a number of other people.

GOING FARTHER

You can follow the Discovery Nature Trail (Route 27) with a short detour to Face Rock to run the full human-features gamut for an additional 0.6 mile (1 km). Or you can continue on past Face Rock to add the Split Rock Loop (Route 28) for a nearly 4.3-mile (6.9 km) roundtrip loop that explores the full extent of the Jumbo Rocks trail network.

27 DISCOVERY NATURE TRAIL

Distance: 0.8 mile (1.3 km)
Elevation gain: 110 feet (35 m)
High point: 4350 feet (1325 m)
Difficulty: Easy
Trail surface: Dirt single-track with a few sections of sandy wash
Maps: USGS 7.5-minute Queen Mountain, Malapai Hill
GPS: 33.997908° N, -116.060084° W
Notes: Day use only; interpretive trail; good for kids, no restroom at trailhead

This trail, a collaboration between Joshua Tree park rangers and students from the Morongo Unified School District, leads you on an easy and informative stroll through a delightful corner of the Jumbo Rocks area. Chief among the rock formations is Face Rock, a towering monolith that bears a striking resemblance to a human profile when viewed from the right angle. Interpretive plaques along the way provide helpful answers to many questions about the landscape.

GETTING THERE

From the North Entrance Station, south of Twentynine Palms, drive south on Park Boulevard for 4.5 miles (7.2 km) to Pinto Wye, and keep right to stay on Park Boulevard. Continue for 2.9 miles (4.7 km) to a pull-out directly across from Skull Rock.

Face Rock is ready for its selfie.

The shared trailhead for Skull Rock Nature Trail and Discovery Nature Trail is on the north side of the road.

ON THE TRAIL

From the shared trailhead with the Skull Rock Nature Trail, keep right to head north on the Discovery Nature Trail. A gentle descent leads you through a short slot canyon before bringing you to a prominent wash at 0.2 mile (0.3 km). At this wash, you reach a junction, with the continuation of the Discovery Nature Trail leading left. Turn right instead for an easy 0.1-mile (0.16 km) detour to Face Rock. You won't be able to identify Face Rock as you approach it, but as soon as you pass the towering granite monolith, turn around for a good look at the face.

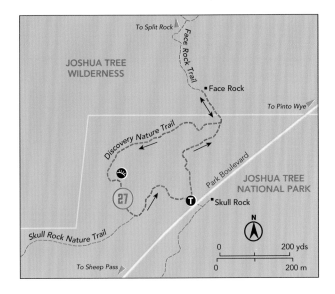

Backtrack to the Discovery Nature Trail, and head west to continue the route. The trail meanders uphill through scenic rock piles before reaching the route's high point around the half-mile (0.8 km) mark. A helpful viewfinder and an interpretive plaque identifying some of the notable geologic features will help you orient yourself to the surrounding landscape. The trail descends from here on a twisting path through a crease between two boulder piles before reaching a junction with the Skull Rock Nature Trail at 0.65 mile (1 km). Turn left to follow the Discovery Nature Trail back to the parking area.

GOING FARTHER

You can combine the Discovery Trail with the Skull Rock Nature Trail (Route 26) for an additional 1.5 miles (2.4 km) of hiking. You can also follow the Face Rock Trail north to join with the Split Rock Trail (Route 28) for an additional 2.3 miles (3.7 km) of hiking.

28 SPLIT ROCK

Distance: 1.9 miles (3.1 km)
Elevation gain: 350 feet (105 m)
High point: 4369 feet (1332 m)
Difficulty: Easy
Trail surface: Dirt single-track trail with occasional granite out-
crops and a few stretches of sandy wash
Map: USGS 7.5-minute Queen Mountain
GPS: 34.009463° N, -116.055732° W
Notes: Day use only; good for kids; pit toilets at trailhead;
picnic area

This undulating trail loops through a gorgeous granite garden
featuring the eponymous Split Rock along with many other
picturesque formations. A number of features will kindle
inspiration for kids and adults alike, although younger ones
may find the route a touch too long to complete under their
own locomotion. A side path leads to Face Rock, one of the
notable anthropomorphic formations in the Jumbo Rocks
area.

GETTING THERE

From the North Entrance Station, south of Twentynine Palms,
drive south on Park Boulevard for 4.5 miles (7.2 km) to Pinto
Wye, and keep right to stay on Park Boulevard. Continue
for 2.2 miles (3.5 km) to a junction with an access road to
the Split Rock Trail on the right. The smooth dirt access
road ends at the trailhead after 0.5 mile (0.8 km). The two
branches of the trail lie on the west end of the parking area,
adjacent to a handful of picnic benches.

ON THE TRAIL

Select the northernmost of the two branches of the Split
Rock Trail to begin a counterclockwise loop. The trail begins

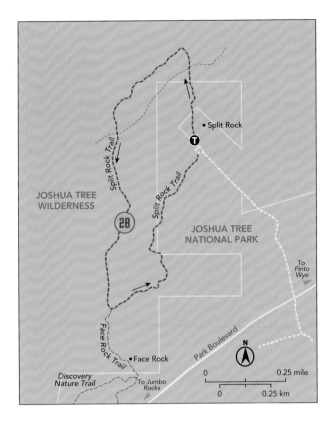

with a moderate descent in the shadow of a large, rugged formation of boulders. After a few hundred yards, the trail reaches a junction with a climber's trail that heads close to the Split Rock formation. From this spot, you'll have a clear view of the monolithic boulder split straight down the middle about a quarter mile to the north.

With the route's primary highlight in the rearview mirror, the trail next drops into a sandy wash before beginning a steady 120-foot ascent (37 m) over 0.25 mile (0.4 km). Solid views compensate for the effort, even though you'll have to

Split Rock

give some of that elevation back as the trail begins undulating into and out of several successive washes carved into the rocky hillside.

The trail keeps up these undulations through granite outcroppings and springtime wildflowers until the 0.8-mile (1.3 km) mark, when it reaches some of the largest boulder piles on the route. Late-evening light brings out the golds and tans in the formations surrounding another sandy wash that runs through the heart of the loop. This wash is a very peaceful place to be as the day draws to a close.

At the southernmost point on the loop, just beyond this wash, a junction with the Face Rock Trail heads south toward Face Rock and beyond to connect with the Discovery Nature Trail. Keep left here to hike north toward the trailhead.

As you descend gently back to the trailhead, you pass through a tiny valley with occasional views east toward the Pinto Mountains. Look for impressive pinyon pines and Muller oaks clinging to water-holding niches within the boulder piles. Marvel at the way these tree species can thrive because their root systems have access to meager pockets of soil within granitic nooks and crannies.

GOING FARTHER

The short diversion south on the Face Rock Trail will bring you to its namesake rock formation at the expense of an additional 0.4 mile (0.6 km) and a modest amount of elevation gain. You can also use the Face Rock Trail to connect to the Discovery Nature Trail (Route 27) and the Skull Rock Nature Trail (Route 26) for an extended exploration of the Jumbo Rocks area.

INDIAN COVE AND NORTH ENTRANCE

This chapter encompasses two slightly different sections of the park that offer a diverse array of experiences. Indian Cove lies on the northern margins of the Wonderland of Rocks, and its topography is dominated by the rugged and photogenic granite formations surrounding the cove. The rest of the trails adjacent to the park's North Entrance, south of the town of Twentynine Palms, lead to destinations as diverse as a lush fan-palm oasis, a historic mine, and a short nature trail to a granite arch.

As this is a relatively quiet section of the park (Fortynine Palms excepted), you will find a bit more solitude than its high-desert areas usually offer. In fact, the park often encourages visitors to use the North Entrance during peak times to avoid traffic congestion. The three campgrounds in this area—Indian Cove, Belle, and White Tank—are also fine alternatives to the sprawling Jumbo Rocks Campground or the competition for campsites at Hidden Valley and Ryan Campgrounds.

OPPOSITE *California fan palms cluster together around permanent water.*

29 INDIAN COVE NATURE TRAIL

Distance: 0.6 mile (1 km)
Elevation gain: 70 feet (20 m)
High point: 3356 feet (1023 m)
Difficulty: Easy
Trail surface: Sand
Map: USGS 7.5-minute Indian Cove
GPS: 34.094880° N, -116.168528° W
Notes: Good for kids; interpretive trail; day use only; pit toilets at trailhead

For an illuminating lesson on the ingenuity of Indian Cove's original inhabitants, follow this short interpretive trail highlighting the many uses of the cove's flora. When you aren't learning about the multiple medicinal uses of creosote or the delectable flavors of desert almond, you can admire the impressive boulder piles that make up the northern ramparts of the Wonderland of Rocks.

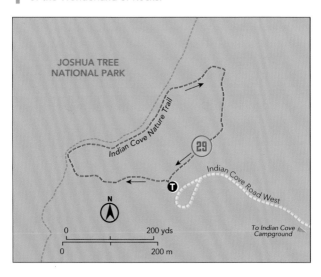

Rugged rock piles and sandy washes in Indian Cove

GETTING THERE

From the junction of Interstate 10 and State Route 62, head north toward Morongo Valley, Yucca Valley, and the town of Joshua Tree for 36.2 miles (58.3 km). Turn right onto Indian Cove Road, and head south for 3 miles (4.8 km) to Indian Cove Campground. Keep right onto Indian Cove Circle and right again onto Indian Cove Road West. The latter smooth dirt road dead-ends at the Indian Cove Nature Trail.

ON THE TRAIL

Follow the short path away from the signed trailhead to the beginning and end of the looping nature trail. Hiking the loop clockwise or counterclockwise has no bearing on the quality of the hike, but let's assume that you're going to turn left for simplicity's sake. After moving away from the trailhead, the trail dips into a major wash draining the Wonderland of Rocks. The trail continues through the wash, meandering northeast for a brief spell before doubling back to the trailhead.

These simple instructions comprise the extent of the routefinding, but you will have a lot of opportunities to stop, learn, and admire, thanks to interpretive plaques placed at regular intervals along the way. Each plaque reveals some aspect of how the indigenous residents of the cove made use of plants that seem to modern eyes innocuous at best and vindictive at worst. The squeamish may balk at the uses to which chuckwallas were put, but a few hungry and open-minded hikers may walk away with a hankering for roasted jackrabbit or poached pencil cholla.

30 RATTLESNAKE CANYON

Distance: 2.2 miles (3.5 km)
Elevation gain: 500 feet (150 m)
High point: 3413 feet (1040 m)
Difficulty: Challenging
Trail surface: Sandy wash, with some steep, rocky sections
Map: USGS 7.5-minute Indian Cove
GPS: 34.085966° N, -116.140166° W
Notes: Navigation required; difficult terrain; day use only; pit toilets at trailhead

The sparse precipitation that falls over the Wonderland of Rocks and the high country around Queen Mountain drains north through a convoluted maze of washes and canyons and then empties into Indian Cove. Before that point, these drainages funnel into Rattlesnake Canyon, a stunning and rugged gash cutting through the northern reaches of the

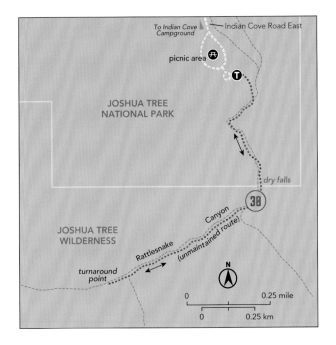

Wonderland. Here, the surface water often flows through the canyon before tumbling over a beautiful, but often dry waterfall.

GETTING THERE

From the junction of Interstate 10 and State Route 62, head north toward Morongo Valley, Yucca Valley, and the town of Joshua Tree for 36.2 miles (58.3 km). Turn right onto Indian Cove Road, and head south for 3 miles (4.8 km) to Indian Cove Campground. At the entrance to the campground, turn left onto Indian Cove Road East, and follow the smooth dirt road until it dead-ends at a series of picnic tables. The informal path into the canyon descends from the uppermost picnic table.

ON THE TRAIL

Rattlesnake Canyon contains exceptionally rugged sections that require steep climbs along granite slabs. These maneuvers are necessary to circumvent a slot canyon and a waterfall, large fields of cavity-pocked slickrock, and countless boulders. If you visit during a very wet season, you may even find yourself wading through knee-deep water. This wicked terrain may be enough to make some hikers move along to the next route, while seasoned desert rats may be licking their chops at the prospect.

Begin by finding a short informal path that descends east from the uppermost picnic tables into a vast wash choked with mesquite and catclaw. Turn due south over a rugged boulder field on the margin of the wash, and look for massive feldspar crystals embedded within many of these boulders. After the wash wraps around a ridge and bends to the southwest, resist the temptation to follow a promising-looking tributary wash directly ahead of you. Instead, follow the main wash as it bends back toward the southeast only to run into a seeming dead end at the base of an often dry waterfall.

This formidable obstacle is the toughest bit of work along the route. Keep to the right of the pools at the base of the falls, and pick your way through jumbles of truck-sized boulders on the right (west). Patience will aid you in fashioning a route through this mess with an eye toward reaching the base of a massive rounded granite slab. The surface of the slab provides better traction than you would suspect, and you can climb it into a vegetation-choked chute that leads to a field of slickrock slabs pocked with water-filled potholes.

The terrain eases up after you work your way over the slabs. Once the wash straightens out and runs due west, continue on soft sand with only the occasional boulder or riparian shrub to impede progress. Even during dry years, you may find water flowing through the wash, and the farther

Endless granite at Rattlesnake Canyon

up-canyon you progress, the more magical the scenery becomes. The papery leaves of cottonwoods and sycamores rattle in the breeze beneath incomprehensibly complex jumbles of boulders that tower hundreds of feet above on either side of the wash. Perhaps most beautiful of all is a large pool filling a depression between house-sized boulders that may come alive with frog croaking and dragonfly buzzing on a cool spring morning.

You can continue up-canyon until the 1.1-mile (1.8 km) mark. At this point, dense brush and formidable boulders preclude progress for all but the most determined.

31 FORTYNINE PALMS OASIS

Distance: 3 miles (4.8 km)
Elevation gain: 750 feet (230 m)
High point: 3075 feet (935 m)
Difficulty: Challenging
Trail surface: Dirt
Map: USGS 7.5-minute Queen Mountain
GPS: 34.119779° N, -116.112281° W
Notes: Day use only; good for older kids; pit toilet at trailhead

> Joshua Tree's most precious commodity was never the gold that ambitious prospectors sought, fought, and sometimes died to obtain. In this arid land, the most valuable substance has always been water. The park's diverse wildlife depends on it, as did human inhabitants dating back to the Pinto people. Abundant amounts of this liquid gold percolate to the surface within Fortynine Palms Canyon, nurturing a beautiful palm grove and providing the lifeblood for the area's fauna.

GETTING THERE

From the town of Joshua Tree at the intersection of Park Boulevard and State Route 62, head east on SR 62 for 10.8 miles (17.4 km) to Canyon Road, and turn right. After 0.9 mile (1.4 km), Canyon Road becomes Fortynine Palms Canyon Road. The road ends at the Fortynine Palms Oasis Trailhead after another 0.9 mile (1.4 km).

ON THE TRAIL

The "challenging" rating for this hike may come as a surprise given the moderate distance and elevation gain. This hike is akin to what your grandparents talked about when they bored you with stories about walking uphill both ways. To reach Fortynine Palms Oasis, you have to climb 300 feet (90 m) over a ridge only to descend 350 feet (105 m) to reach

Sweet, beautiful, blissful shade

the oasis. According to the ancient hiking adage "What goes down must come back up," the steep climb back to this trailhead will likely occur during a warmer part of the day. I therefore encourage you not to underestimate this hike's difficulty. Young children may not appreciate the sunny climb out of the canyon, but I have observed numerous older kids handling the climb admirably.

The Fortynine Palms Oasis Trail leads south from the parking lot on a moderate incline. The trail soon veers to the southeast while making occasional switchbacks as it works its way to the crest of Fortynine Palms Canyon at 0.7 mile (1.1 km). From this point, it's a downhill walk to the oasis, which you can spot off in the distance.

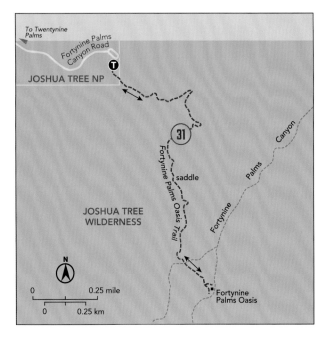

As you cross into Fortynine Palms Canyon, the route descends obliquely along a rocky hillside cut by occasional ravines and washes. You'll have a great chance of spotting chuckwallas, large lizards with a passion for sunbathing, as they bask on rock outcrops. The trail bottoms out at 1.5 miles (2.4 km) at the foot of the oasis. Whether there are precisely forty-nine palms is unlikely, and the grove looks much bigger than the number suggests. A pair of spur trails leads you through a corner of the grove to a spot overlooking a large pool. Another trail looks over the heart of the grove and its enticing shade.

As much as you may want to find a flat rock tucked under that deep shade, be mindful of the signs warning you to not approach the grove due to its biological sensitivity. The springs are a vital water source for resident bighorn sheep, an endangered species that doesn't react well to a lot of humans cavorting near its water supply. Please respect the signs and avoid entering the grove.

32 CONTACT MINE

Distance: 3.8 miles (6.1 km)
Elevation gain: 725 feet (220 m)
High point: 3628 feet (1106 m)
Difficulty: Moderate
Trail surface: Sandy wash, then rocky dirt road
Map: USGS 7.5-minute Queen Mountain
GPS: 34.072509° N, -116.032878° W
Notes: Day use only; minor navigation required; no restroom at trailhead

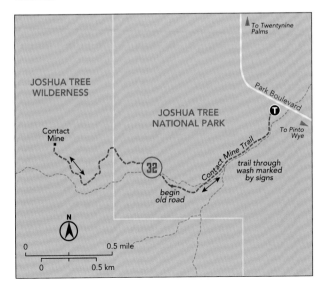

When the longer, warmer days of spring herald the end of the winter rainy season, wildflowers burst forth in profusion in virtually every nook and cranny of the transition zone between the Mojave and Colorado Deserts. Pick a time during late March and early April—especially following a solid season of rain—to experience impressive wildflower displays of brittlebush, desert chicory, phacelias, poppies, and mallows. Cap the hike off with a visit to an abandoned mine at the end of an impressively constructed former mining road.

GETTING THERE

From the North Entrance Station, south of Twentynine Palms, head south on Park Boulevard for 0.5 mile (0.8 km) to the Contact Mine Trailhead on the west (right) side of the road.

ON THE TRAIL

The initial section of the trail features bright-red markers spaced at regular intervals that guide hikers through the wash to the beginning of the old mining road. The signs are impossible to miss, but even if you are following them, try to keep to the left (south) side of the wash so as not to miss the place where you leave the wash and begin following the old road at 0.8 mile (1.3 km).

Contact Mine offers supreme solitude.

When you reach the beginning of the old road, follow it up onto a low ridge and continue as the road parallels the wash to the north. Cross into the wash one more time at 1 mile (1.6 km) and then begin a moderate climb into and out of a ravine. After cresting a low saddle at 1.4 miles (2.3 km), the road rounds a bend to approach the Contact Mine. The slopes on the left and right side of the road are carpeted with brittlebush, a member of the daisy family that produces clusters of brilliant yellow blossoms during the spring. Closer afoot, numerous annuals brighten up the edges of the road.

The trail becomes fairly rocky on the approach, and a couple of diverging paths present possible routes to the mine. Both paths end up at the mine, which includes three barricaded mine shafts and the usual detritus of rusted-out mining equipment, plus the remnants of an old railroad track. Even if you visit before wildflower season or after a dry winter, the mine is a fascinating area to explore. Better yet, there's an appreciable amount of solitude in this quiet corner of the park, which may be the best reward of all.

33 ARCH ROCK NATURE TRAIL

Distance: 0.5 mile (0.8 km)
Elevation gain: 50 feet (15 m)
High point: 3845 feet (1170 m)
Difficulty: Easy
Trail surface: Sand and sporadic rock outcrops
Map: USGS 7.5-minute Queen Mountain
GPS: 33.985373° N, -116.016691° W
Notes: Day use only; good for kids; interpretive trail; restroom adjacent to trailhead within campground

As you head south from Pinto Wye toward Pinto Basin, the last of Joshua Tree's famous monzogranite boulder piles

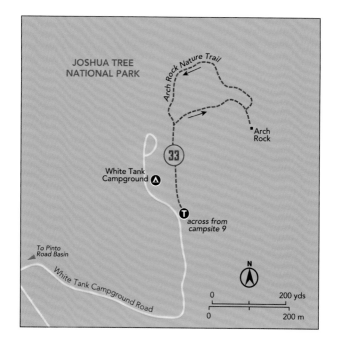

punctuate the high-desert valleys before vanishing at the Mojave-Colorado transition zone. The Arch Rock Nature Trail explores one of the last of these boulder piles, which includes an impressive arch set within an equally impressive boulder garden. Kids will love the opportunities for easy scrambling, and photographers will have numerous subjects to consider among the boulder fields.

GETTING THERE

From the North Entrance Station, south of Twentynine Palms, head south on Park Boulevard for 4.6 miles (7.4 km) to Pinto Wye. Turn left onto Pinto Basin Road, and continue south for another 2.7 miles (4.3 km) to the entrance of White Tank Campground on the left side of the road. Turn left into the campground, and continue into the campground for 0.2 mile (0.3 km) to a parking area across from campsite 9.

ON THE TRAIL

Head north from the signed trailhead along a wide sandy path marked at intervals with interpretive plaques that explain the origins of the surrounding granite formations. After 100 yards (90 m), the trail splits at a Y junction into two looping branches. Turn right and climb over a low rise to drop down toward a junction with a spur trail leading to Arch Rock. Keep right at this junction to reach the base of the arch at 0.2 mile (0.3 km).

Not only is the arch a beautiful formation, but many of the formations surrounding the arch are beautiful in a less ostentatious way. When you've seen all you wish to see around the arch, return to the main trail and turn right to complete the loop walking counterclockwise. At 0.4 mile (0.6 km), return to the Y junction for an easy 100-yard walk back to your car.

Arch Rock in the early morning

PINTO BASIN AND COTTONWOOD SPRING

The illusion of Joshua Tree as a benign playground full of boulder piles and Seussian trees melts away under the searing desert sun the moment you pass through the transition zone between the Mojave and Colorado Deserts. Here in the low desert, the boulder piles and Joshua trees vanish. In their place, you will find a more wicked assortment of cholla, ocotillo, and jagged ridges and hillsides riddled with a bewildering variety of rock types.

If this prospect makes you want to turn around and head straight back to Lost Horse Valley, look more closely. The low desert may not have the star power of the Wonderland of Rocks, but it provides a deep, varied, and forceful array of experiences all its own. In this superficially stark landscape, you will find lush springs and palm groves. You'll find silence and simplicity in endless desert washes. You'll experience the thrill of scaling a barren ridge to find yourself high above a seemingly infinite landscape.

Services are more limited around Pinto Basin and Cottonwood Spring. A single campground at Cottonwood Spring is the only formal lodging available, although backcountry trailheads at Turkey Flat, Porcupine Wash, and Cottonwood Spring enable deeper explorations into the vast low-desert landscape.

OPPOSITE *Sunrises at Porcupine Wash are stunning.*

34 CHOLLA CACTUS GARDEN

Distance: 0.3 mile (0.5 km)
Elevation gain: Negligible
High point: 2202 feet (671 m)
Difficulty: Easy
Trail surface: Dirt
Map: USGS 7.5-minute Fried Liver Wash
GPS: 33.925536° N, -115.928895° W
Notes: Day use only; interpretive trail; no restroom at trailhead

One of botanists' crueler jokes was the nicknaming of the most sinister plant in California after something that everybody loves to hug. This short nature loop explores a large patch of teddy bear cholla (a.k.a. jumping cholla) in a macabre hiking version of the children's game "don't touch the lava," with cactus spines replacing the lava. With an introduction like that, you might wonder why you'd bother wandering through a patch of plants that would love to make you hurt.

Stop by on a cool early morning as the rising desert sun illuminates each vindictive needle in a warm glow. At times like that, you'll forgive this teddy bear for its cruelty—unless you're careless enough to make a closer acquaintance.

GETTING THERE

From the North Entrance Station, south of Twentynine Palms, head south on Park Boulevard for 4.6 miles (7.4 km) to Pinto Wye. Turn left onto Pinto Basin Road, and continue south for another 9.9 miles (15.9 km) to the Cholla Cactus Garden Nature Trail on the right (west) side of the road.

ON THE TRAIL

This short interpretive trail loops through a dense thicket of teddy bear cholla and several of its slightly less-sinister relatives, including pencil cholla and silver cholla. The 0.3-mile

Keep toddlers close by in this garden.

(0.5 km) loop is simple to follow, and a pamphlet, available at the trailhead or at one of the visitor centers, highlights some of the resident flora and adds a deeper appreciation for low-desert plants. Despite the dangerous nature of these plants, they are quite beautiful in the way they reflect and refract light. Early mornings and late afternoons are the best times to be here. Early birds get the reward of watching the sun rise over Pinto Basin to the east, along with the warm glow of illuminated cholla spines.

Usually, routes of this length are perfect for children, but this is the last place in the park that you want to let your

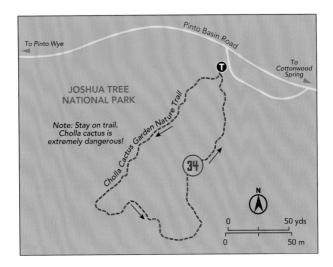

children run free. Cholla spines conceal tiny barbs that have no trouble penetrating skin. Once it gets into the skin, the barb keeps the spine buried in the skin. The cholla pods, which are littered around the base of the cacti, attach at the slightest contact, and it takes very little for a cholla pod to attach to your ankle. Once in, the best way to get it out is to use a comb to pull the pod from the skin. Then you need to use pliers to pull out each individual spine. If you have toddlers, you're probably already having nightmares about this trail. For parents, children, and everyone else, it is imperative that you keep to the trail!

35 PINTO MOUNTAIN

Distance: 9.2 miles (14.8 km)
Elevation gain: 2850 feet (870 m)
High point: 3983 feet (1214 m)
Difficulty: Strenuous

Trail surface: Flat, sandy desert, followed by a faint use trail up a rocky ridge
Map: USGS 7.5-minute Pinto Mountain
GPS: 33.902355° N, -115.834952° W
Notes: Suitable for backpacking; backcountry registration board at trailhead; navigation required; difficult terrain; no restroom at trailhead

> This challenging cross-country hike traverses the vast expanse of Pinto Basin to follow a rocky, colorful ridgeline to the high point of the Pinto Mountains. A fascinating mélange of rock types color the ridgeline in a surprising variety of hues, while the massive, flat summit makes both a great spot to soak in endless desert views as well as an unforgettable, windswept backpacking destination.

GETTING THERE

Take exit 168 on Interstate 10 for Cottonwood Springs Road heading north to Twentynine Palms, and drive north on Cottonwood Springs Road for 6.7 miles (10.8 km), which then becomes Pinto Basin Road. Continue for another 13.7 miles (22 km) to the Turkey Flat Trail on the right (north) side of the road.

California barrel cacti add colorful punctuation to the stark slopes of Pinto Mountain.

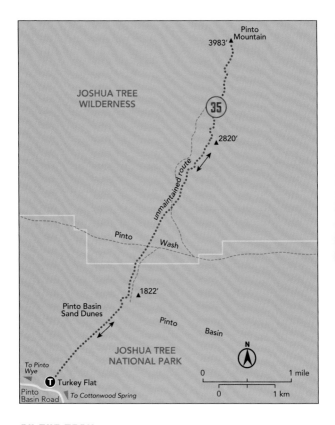

ON THE TRAIL

From the Turkey Flat Trailhead, set out across open desert heading due northeast across Pinto Basin toward a low, sandy ridge 1.1 miles (1.8 km) from the trailhead. This sandy ridge is one of the Pinto Basin sand dunes, although it is not a true sand dune. These dunes are gravelly ridges upon which sand has accumulated. Be on the lookout for thickets of fragrant sand verbena during the spring.

Once you reach the dune, climb up and over and then drop into a wash that runs north just west of peak 1822 on

Smoke tree in the morning light in Pinto Basin

your topo map (1.5 miles, 2.4 km). Once the wash passes that peak, it empties into open desert. The flat, easily identified high point of Pinto Mountain lies to the northeast. Below the peak, you can see a deep canyon cut into the mountain's southern flank. Set a course directly for the ridge on the right side of this canyon.

After climbing up the canyon's rocky alluvial fan, you reach the foot of the ridge at 2.7 miles. Find the use trail that scales the ridge, and commence a rocky uphill climb. The first 0.5 mile (0.8 km) of the climb is rather steep on occasionally loose talus. Trekking poles will come in handy in helping you keep your footing. At several spots, you will want to stick close to the use trail as it skirts occasional rock outcrops along the ridge.

The grade eases somewhat around the 2400-foot (730 m) contour. This spot also coincides with the beginning of several alternating bands of white and pink quartz and darker metamorphic gneiss.

At 3.4 miles (5.5 km), the trail passes through a shallow valley below peak 2820, losing a bit of elevation before recommencing the climb over more alternating bands of quartz and gneiss. Sporadic barrel cacti add splashes of red with yellow blossoms during the spring.

The toughest part of the climb awaits at 3.9 miles (6.3 km). This part of the route gains 950 feet (290 m) over a mere 0.5 mile (0.8 km), and a lot of it takes place on loose, rocky surfaces. As tortuous as this climb is, you can look forward to a gentle ascent to the large, flat summit at 4.4 miles (7.1 km). At a large rock pile marking the summit at 4.6 miles (7.4 km), you can finally catch your breath for good while you enjoy the sweeping views.

Below you and looking south, scan the spacious entirety of Pinto Basin bound by the Pinto, Coxcomb, Eagle, and Hexie Mountains. The low-density sprawl of Twentynine Palms unfurls north toward the Marine Corps base. Views west take in both Mount San Gorgonio and Mount San Jacinto, as well as high points like Queen Mountain, Ryan Mountain, and Quail Mountain.

Backpackers can camp anywhere within Pinto Basin, provided they're at least a mile (1.6 km) from the trailhead. Really adventurous backpackers can schlep all of their gear and extra water to the summit, where a number of flat spots perfect for camping are scattered around the summit plateau. As remarkable as these camping spots are, be prepared for the possibility of terrific winds—especially during the spring.

On the return journey, you may find it difficult to stick to the exact path that you took toward the summit. Expect to continue the same kind of small-scale routefinding you enjoyed on the way up. Also, be sure to take a deliberate pace on the descent. It may be tempting to hustle back down the mountain, but the unforgiving terrain can create opportunities for injury if you aren't careful.

36 PORCUPINE WASH AND RUBY LEE WELL

Distance: 7.7 miles (12.4 km)

Elevation gain: 770 feet (235 m)

High point: 3081 feet (939 m)

Difficulty: Challenging

Trail surface: Sandy washes with a few sections of walking across open desert

Map: USGS 7.5-minute Porcupine Wash

GPS: 33.846069° N, -115.777624° W

Notes: Suitable for backpacking; backcountry registration board at trailhead; navigation required; moderate terrain; no restroom at trailhead; historical interest

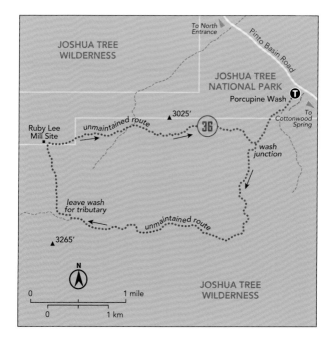

The beds at the Ruby Lee Mill homestead site are terrible, but at least the views are pretty good.

Dust off the map and compass for a satisfying jaunt through a prominent wash draining the eastern end of the Hexie Mountains, and hike cross-country to connect with a historic mill site in a secluded valley. Gorgeous scenery and abundant solitude provide the perfect anecdote for hikers weary of the more congested corners of the park. This route is a great option for hikers looking for an easier backpacking option in Joshua Tree.

GETTING THERE

Take exit 168 on Interstate 10 for Cottonwood Springs Road heading north to Twentynine Palms and drive north on Cottonwood Springs Road for 6.7 miles (10.8 km), which then becomes Pinto Basin Road. Continue for another 8.5 miles (13.7 km) to the Porcupine Wash Trailhead on the left (west) side of the road.

ON THE TRAIL

Even though an inviting path leads away from the back-country registration board, avoid that trail as it would pull you away from your true bearing toward Porcupine Wash. Instead, walk north along the shoulder of Pinto Basin Road for about 20 yards (18 m) and then turn left to follow the wash southwest. After 0.7 mile (1.1 km) of walking through the gradually narrowing wash, you arrive at a split, where a tributary wash joins from the west. Keep left here to continue following Porcupine Wash, but commit this spot to memory. The tributary wash will be your return route.

Continue through Porcupine Wash as it twists through a narrow, meandering canyon that leads south. At 2 miles (3.2 km), the wash turns west and broadens into a wide valley. At 3 miles (4.8 km), the valley narrows into a canyon before widening again at 3.7 miles (6 km). When the wash widens for the second time, keep to the right side of this valley and search for a prominent tributary wash feeding the main wash from the north at 3.9 miles (6.3 km). Turn right into this wash, and climb up and over a short rocky section to continue nearly due north across a valley toward the Ruby Lee Well site at the northern end of the valley at 4.6 miles (7.4 km). Note that the topo map shows the site 0.1 mile (0.2 km) west of its true location.

The mill site served the Ruby Lee Mine claimed by Ruby Lee Rule in 1936. The limited records about activity in the mines reveal no concrete information about how productive the mine was or how long the mill operated. However, you will find a relatively complex cabin constructed against a rock outcrop a few yards south of the well. A large boulder inscribed with the words "Ruby Lee 1935 Mill Site" stands above the well.

Older topo maps indicate the presence of an old jeep road leading from the mill site all the way back to Pinto Basin

Road. Only faint hints of this road remain between the mill and the aforementioned tributary wash leading back to Porcupine Wash. Rather than wasting a lot of time trying to find and stick to that road, simply head east along the base of the low hills on the north side of the valley.

At 5.6 miles (9 km), you'll cross a large wash draining the valley. At this point, you may spot the occasional cairn marking a trace of the old jeep road as you continue up and over the ridge defining the wash's eastern boundary. The cairns continue to mark a more defined stretch of the jeep trail beyond the wash, and from here the road parallels another wash that runs east for about a quarter mile (0.4 km). At that point, the road once again disappears, and joining the wash you had been paralleling is your best bet. Although you may be able to locate more sections of the jeep road, save yourself the trouble and follow the wash over a few initial rocky sections until it flattens out and bends south back to Porcupine Wash at 7 miles (11.3 km).

Once you're back in Porcupine Wash, it's a 0.7-mile (1.1 km) walk northeast back to your car at Pinto Basin Road.

37 MASTODON PEAK

Distance: 2.8 miles (4.5 km)
Elevation gain: 500 feet (150 m)
High point: 3370 feet (1025 m)
Difficulty: Moderate
Trail surface: Sand with occasional rocky patches
Map: USGS 7.5-minute Cottonwood Spring
GPS: 33.737007° N, -115.810662° W
Notes: Day use only; good for kids; backcountry registration board and restroom at trailhead; historical interest

Truck-sized boulder cleaved in two

This perfect introduction to the Cottonwood Spring area is a moderate loop suitable for just about everybody. The route visits the easily accessible summit, passes by a pair of historic mining sites, revels in a brief patch of cool shade at Cottonwood Spring, and takes in colorful wildflower displays during late winter and early spring.

GETTING THERE

Take exit 168 on Interstate 10 for Cottonwood Springs Road heading north to Twentynine Palms and drive north on Cottonwood Springs Road for 6.8 miles (10.9 km). Then turn right onto Cottonwood Oasis Road. Follow Cottonwood Oasis Road for 1.2 miles (1.9 km) to the parking area and Cottonwood Spring Trailhead.

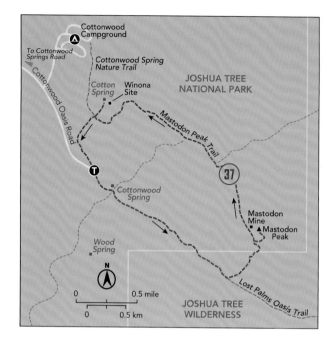

ON THE TRAIL

Set out from the signed trailhead and begin with a short walk downhill to a lush copse of Fremont cottonwoods and California fan palms clustered around the perennial spring that was once an important water source for the indigenous Cahuilla people. A few bedrock mortars (*morteros*) just east of the spring testify to the activity of the Cahuilla. They used these *morteros* to pound and grind seeds and nuts into flour to be made into porridge and tortilla-like cakes.

After the spring, the trail settles into a moderate climb through a broad ravine toward a junction with the Mastodon Peak Trail at 0.7 mile (1.1 km). Turn left at this junction and begin a rocky, sometimes twisting climb through another ravine that tops out at the base of Mastodon Peak at 1 mile (1.6 km). Along the way, you'll note several intriguing rock formations that might divert you for a bit of casual exploration.

To reach Mastodon Peak, follow the rocky, unmaintained trail that's as much a scramble as it is a footpath. Younger kids may struggle with the climb, but older kids who are adept at this sort of maneuvering will have little trouble. The summit views take in a broad slice of the immediate terrain, with the dark, undulating ridge of the Santa Rosa Mountains basking in a blue haze off in the distance. If the atmospheric clarity is sufficient, you'll also have a good view of the Salton Sea. Turn north, and you'll get a fine look at the rugged Eagle Mountains.

Backtrack from the peak, and continue west on the loop. You immediately reach the Mastodon Mine on the western base of the peak at 1.2 miles (1.9 km). The Hulsey family established this fairly well-preserved mine and pursued bullion by way of a vein of quartz. However, the underlying geology eventually thwarted their attempt to extract the bulk of the gold.

Continue past the mine on a westward course as the route crosses over a low ridge before dropping into a wide sandy wash at 1.5 miles (2.4 km). The trail pulls away from the wash

Looking south toward the Salton Sea from Mastodon Peak

0.2 mile (0.3 km) later to climb over another low ridge before dropping into another wash. Just after the wash bends to the south, the trail climbs out of the wash once again and then drops down to a junction with the Cottonwood Spring Nature Trail at 2.2 miles (3.5 km).

When you reach the Cottonwood Spring Nature Trail, you can also follow a short spur trail north from the junction toward a small grove of trees, including some non-native eucalyptus, that marks the site of the village of Winona. Winona held the stamping mill that processed the gold, as well as housing for the people who worked the mine. Most of the structures are gone, but a few concrete foundations remain.

Return to the Cottonwood Spring Nature Trail that follows (you guessed it) another wash leading you back to the parking lot. Along the way, you can peruse some but not all of the nature trail's interpretive plaques describing Cahuilla food sources in the area. Avoid turning right toward the campground, unless you want to see the remaining information plaques along the Cottonwood Spring Nature Trail.

GOING FARTHER

You can combine Routes 37 and 38 (Lost Palms Oasis) for an 8.5-mile (13.7 km) roundtrip hike that gains and loses 1600 feet. The easiest way to combine the two is to hike to Lost Palms Oasis and then turn right onto the Mastodon Peak Trail on the return journey. From there, you can follow the Mastodon Peak Loop back to your car.

38 LOST PALMS OASIS

Distance: 7.2 miles (11.6 km)
Elevation gain: 1400 feet (425 m)
High point: 3446 feet (1050 m)
Difficulty: Challenging

California fan palms show off their shaggy beards at Lost Palms Oasis.

The convoluted beauty of Lost Palms Canyon

Trail surface: Mostly hard-packed sand with occasional soft sand within washes
Map: USGS 7.5-minute Cottonwood Spring
GPS: 33.737007° N, -115.810662° W
Notes: Suitable for backpacking (camping prohibited in day-use area surrounding palms); backcountry registration board and restroom at trailhead; historical interest

This popular route leads you to the largest grove of California fan palms in the park. Along the way, you pass through middle-elevation desert terrain that's been sliced, diced, folded, molded, bent, and often broken by the nearby San Andreas Fault. Occasional vistas south into the Salton Trough, which includes the Salton Sea set against the dusky ridge of the Santa Rosa Mountains, add interest along the way.

GETTING THERE

Take exit 168 on Interstate 10 for Cottonwood Springs Road heading north to Twentynine Palms and drive north on Cottonwood Springs Road for 6.8 miles (10.9 km), then turn right onto Cottonwood Oasis Road. Follow Cottonwood Oasis Road for 1.2 miles (1.9 km) to the parking area and Cottonwood Spring Trailhead.

ON THE TRAIL

For a hike that stays between an elevation range of 2950 and 3446 feet (900 and 1050 km), this route gains and loses a surprising amount of elevation (1400 feet; 425 km). This seemingly inflated number is the result of the trail traversing a landscape that is rarely ever content to remain flat.

This convoluted rising and falling is a consequence of close proximity to the San Andreas Fault. Many people know this fault as the earthquake-inducing monster that will one day turn California into an island. This is, of course, not true. In actuality, the fault will slowly push Southern California north past San Francisco after millions of years. The more immediate effect of the fault has been to crumple the landscape

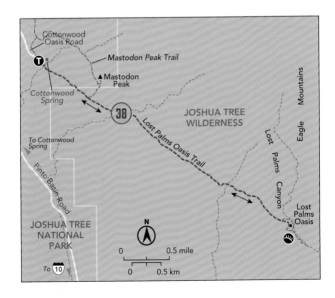

like a used-up piece of paper. This is all to say that you can expect to go up and down a lot on your way to the palms.

Set out from the parking area and reach Cottonwood Spring after a short 0.1-mile (0.16 km) downhill walk. After stopping briefly to bask in that rarest of desert unicorns—shade—continue past the spring on an uphill climb that reaches a junction with the Mastodon Peak Trail at 0.7 mile (1.1 km). Stay straight at this junction and settle into a prolonged but gentle ascent that picks up about 300 feet (90 m) over the next 1.5 miles (2.4 km).

You won't encounter any junctions or choices for the remainder of the route, which allows you to enjoy the beautiful rolling terrain. However, be sure to stick to the trail as the terrain gets confusing in a hurry if you wander off. Wildflowers tend to grace the usually beige landscape with bursts of improbable color during the late-winter and early-spring months. An interesting mixture of perennial shrubs and cacti representing both the high-desert and low-desert realms overlap here. You'll see ocotillo, a hallmark specimen of the Colorado Desert, along with California juniper, a herald of the high-desert realm, at different points along the trail.

After much rising and falling into washes and over ridges, the trail crests one final ridge at 3 miles (4.8 km) and begins the descent to Lost Palms Oasis by way of a ruggedly beautiful canyon. At 3.5 miles (5.6 km), the official trail ends at a viewpoint overlooking the clusters of stately fan palms that form the oasis in the canyon below and the slopes just to the north. A pair of use trails drop into this canyon to form a makeshift loop connected by Lost Palms Canyon's wash that allows you to get an up-close look at the palms.

As with any route that gains and loses a lot of elevation along the way, be aware that the return journey will tax your energy nearly as much as the approach. The tougher trip back may oblige you to walk uphill at a hotter part of the day, which will also tax your body.

GOING FARTHER

You can combine the Mastodon Peak Loop (Route 37) with this route to create an 8.5-mile (13.7 km) roundtrip hike with 1600 feet (490 m) of elevation gain and loss. On the return journey from the oasis, turn right onto the Mastodon Peak Trail, and follow the Mastodon Peak Loop back to your starting point.

APPENDIX A: CONTACT INFORMATION

Black Rock Nature Center

Open: October through May; Daily (except Friday) 8:00 AM to 4:00 PM; Fridays 8:00 AM to 8:00 PM

Location: 9800 Black Rock Canyon Road, Yucca Valley, CA 92284; within Black Rock Campground

Phone: 760-367-3001

Cottonwood Visitor Center

Open: Daily 8:30 AM to 4:00 PM

Location: Pinto Basin Road, Twentynine Palms, CA 92277

Phone: 760-367-5500

Indian Cove Ranger Station

Open: Daily 8:00 AM to 5:00 PM

Location: Indian Cove Road, Twentynine Palms, CA 92277

Phone: 760-367-5500

Joshua Tree Visitor Center

Open: Daily 8:00 AM to 5:00 PM

Location: 6554 Park Boulevard, Joshua Tree, CA 92256; north of the park's West Entrance Station and just south of State Route 62

Phone: 760-366-1855

OPPOSITE *The union of water, granite, and clear blue skies is what desert hikers' dreams are made of.*

Oasis Visitor Center and Park Headquarters

Open: 8:30 AM to 5:00 PM

Location: 74485 National Park Drive, Twentynine Palms, CA 92277; adjacent to Oasis of Mara in Twentynine Palms

Phone: 760-367-5500

ASSOCIATED AGENCIES

Joshua Tree National Park Association

Official park partner

www.joshuatree.org

Location: 74485 National Park Drive, Twentynine Palms, CA 92277

Phone: 760-367-5535

PUBLIC TRANSPORTATION

The RoadRunner Shuttle

www.jtnproadrunner.org

CAMPGROUNDS

Belle Campground

Location: On Pinto Basin Road, 1.3 miles (2.1 km) south of Pinto Wye

Seasons: Year round

Number of sites: 18

Reservations: First come, first served

Amenities: Trash/recycling collection, vault toilets

Black Rock Campground

Location: 9800 Black Rock Canyon Road, Yucca Valley, CA 92284

Seasons: Year round

Number of sites: 99

Reservations: October through May via Recreation.gov; first come, first served rest of year

Voluptuous monzogranite formations cut by cross-jointing at Jumbo Rocks

Amenities: Cell reception, trash/recycling collection, amphitheater, staff on-site, dump station, potable water, flush toilets, nearby equestrian camping

Cottonwood Campground
Location: On Pinto Basin Road, 6.7 miles (10.8 km) north of Interstate 10
Seasons: Year round
Number of sites: 62 (3 group sites)
Reservations: October through May via Recreation.gov; first come, first served rest of year
Amenities: Trash/recycling collection, amphitheater, dump station, potable water, flush toilets

Hidden Valley Campground
Location: On Park Boulevard, 10 miles (16 km) east of the West Entrance
Seasons: Year round
Number of sites: 44
Reservations: First come, first served
Amenities: Trash/recycling collection, vault toilets

Indian Cove Campground

Location: 9 miles (14.5 km) east from the intersection of Park Boulevard and State Route 62; 3.2 miles (5.1 km) south on Indian Cove Road

Seasons: Year round

Number of sites: 101 (13 group sites)

Reservations: October through May via Recreation.gov; first come, first served rest of year

Amenities: Trash/recycling collection, staff on-site (seasonal), amphitheater, vault toilets

Jumbo Rocks Campground

Location: On Park Boulevard, 17.3 miles (27.8 km) east of the West Entrance; 8.1 miles (13 km) south of the North Entrance

Seasons: Year round

Number of sites: 124

Reservations: October through May via Recreation.gov; first come, first served rest of year

Amenities: Trash/recycling collection, amphitheater, vault toilets

Ryan Campground

Location: On Park Boulevard, 11 miles (18 km) east of the West Entrance

Seasons: Year round (equestrian campsites closed during the summer)

Number of sites: 31

Reservations: First come, first served

Amenities: Trash/recycling collection, vault toilets

Sheep Pass Group Campground

Location: On Park Boulevard, 13.3 miles (21.4 km) east of the West Entrance

Seasons: Year round

Number of sites: 6 group sites

Reservations: Year round through Recreation.gov

Amenities: Trash/recycling collection, vault toilets

White Tank Campground

Location: On Pinto Basin Road, 2.7 miles (4.3 km) south of Pinto Wye

Seasons: Year round

Number of sites: 15

Reservations: First come, first served

Amenities: Trash/recycling collection, vault toilets

APPENDIX B:
FURTHER READING

GEOLOGY

Eggers, Margaret R., ed. *Mining History and Geology of Joshua Tree National Park*. San Diego: San Diego Association of Geologists, 2004.

Sharp, Robert P., and Allen F. Glazner. *Geology Underfoot in Southern California*. Missoula, MT: Mountain Press Publishing, 1993.

Trent, D. D., and R. W. Hazlett. *Joshua Tree National Park Geology*. Twentynine Palms, CA: Joshua Tree National Park Association, 2002.

BIOLOGY

Babb, Randall D. *Reptiles and Amphibians of the Mojave Desert: A Guide to Common and Notable Species*. Boynton Beach, FL: Quick Reference Publishing, 2014.

Jorgensen, Mark C. *Desert Bighorn Sheep: Wilderness Icon*. El Cajon, CA: Sunbelt Publications, 2014.

Peterson, Roger T. *Peterson Field Guide to Birds of Western North America*. 4th ed. New York: Peterson Field Guides, 2010.

Schoenherr, Allan A. *A Natural History of California*. 2nd ed. Berkeley: University of California Press, 2017.

Taylor, Ronald J. *Desert Wildflowers of North America*. Missoula, MT: Mountain Press Publishing, 1998.

HISTORY

Clapp, Nicholas. *Gold and Silver in the Mojave*. El Cajon, CA: Sunbelt Publications, 2012.

Kidwell, Art. *Ambush: The Story of Bill Keys*. Twentynine Palms, CA: Desert Moon Press, 1995.

Lightfoot, Kent G., and Otis Parrish. *California Indians and Their Environment: An Introduction*. Berkeley: University of California Press, 2009.

Zarki, Joseph W. *Images of America: Joshua Tree National Park*. Mount Pleasant, SC: Arcadia Publishing, 2015.

ROCK CLIMBING

Gaines, Bob. *Best Climbs: Joshua Tree National Park*. Helena, MT: Falcon Guides, 2012.

Vogel, Randy. *Rock Climbing Joshua Tree*. 2nd ed. Guilford, CT: Globe Pequot Press, 2000.

ASTRONOMY

Nordgren, Tyler. *Stars Above, Earth Below: A Guide to Astronomy in the National Parks*. Chichester, England: Praxis Publishing, 2010.

Schneider, Howard. *A Backyard Guide to the Night Sky*. Des Moines, IA: National Geographic, 2009.

MISCELLANEOUS

Alloway, David. *Desert Survival Skills*. Austin: University of Texas Press, 2000.

Burns, Bob, and Mike Burns. *Wilderness Navigation: Finding Your Way Using Map, Compass, Altimeter, and GPS*. 3rd ed. Seattle: Mountaineers Books, 2015.

ACKNOWLEDGMENTS

Thanks first and foremost to my wife, Kelly, for supporting me in taking this book on and not minding that I disappear into the wild for several days at a time. I hope it's not because I smell bad. Thanks to my son, Hank, not necessarily because you helped me write this book, but because you're just so damn cute and funny. Thanks also to my friend Kyle Kuns for joining me on some of the fieldwork. Thanks to my friend Shawnté Salabert for suggesting that I pursue this project and for putting in a good word for me. I feel like I can never stop thanking Casey Schreiner enough for giving me a chance to write about trails in the first place.

Special thanks to Kate Rogers and Laura Shauger for patiently fielding my questions and offering valuable constructive criticism. Thanks also to the rest of the Mountaineers Books team behind the production of this book, including Jen Grable, McKenzie Long, and Bart Wright. And finally, thanks to the park employees and individuals and agencies associated with the park, not just for their help in making sure I got the information in this book right, but for their tireless efforts in protecting this fragile wonderland.

OPPOSITE *A Joshua tree's prayers are answered by a fading sunset.*

INDEX

ABOUT THE AUTHOR

Scott Turner is a native Californian hiking guide author who moonlights as a marriage and family therapist. When he isn't helping families and individuals through mental health challenges, he's exploring the American West's most beautiful places on foot. His writing credits include a revision and update of Jerry Schad's "hiking Bible" for San Diego, *Afoot & Afield: San Diego County*. He has also contributed more than 250 trail descriptions across Southern California, the Sierra Nevada, Hawaii, Utah, Arizona, and Montana for Modern Hiker, the West's most widely read hiking website.

This is his first of (hopefully) many books for Mountaineers Books. Scott is working on guides to Zion and Bryce and to Sequoia–Kings Canyon in the Hike the Parks series. Learn more about him at https://onethousandmilesblog.wordpress.com.

Scott lives in sunny Carlsbad, California, with his wife, Kelly, his son, Hank, and his cat, Dingleberry.

MOUNTAINEERS BOOKS, including its two imprints, Skipstone and Braided River, is a leading publisher of quality outdoor recreation, sustainability, and conservation titles. As a 501(c)(3) nonprofit, we are committed to supporting the environmental and educational goals of our organization by providing expert information on human-powered adventure, sustainable practices at home and on the trail, and preservation of wilderness.

Our publications are made possible through the generosity of donors, and through sales of more than 700 titles on outdoor recreation, sustainable lifestyle, and conservation. To donate, purchase books, or learn more, visit us online:

MOUNTAINEERS BOOKS

1001 SW Klickitat Way, Suite 201 • Seattle, WA 98134 • 800-553-4453
mbooks@mountaineersbooks.org • www.mountaineersbooks.org

An independent nonprofit publisher since 1960

Leave No Trace strives to educate visitors about the nature of their recreational impacts and offers techniques to prevent and minimize such impacts. Leave No Trace is best understood as an educational and ethical program, not as a set of rules and regulations. For more information, visit www.lnt.org or call 800-332-4100.

YOU MAY ALSO LIKE